I0110855

Overpowering
Influence
of the
Truth

Edward Franklin Eberly

This book is a work of non-fiction. Unless otherwise noted, the author and the publisher make no explicit guarantees as to the accuracy of the information contained in this book and in some cases, names of people and places have been altered to protect their privacy.

Copyright © 2013 by Edward Franklin Eberly

No part of this book may be reproduced, stored in a retrieval system, or transmitted by any means without the written permission of the author.

All Scripture quotations are taken from the King James Version.

ISBN: 978-0-615-76770-3

Printed in the United States of America

Visit our Website at: www.extendedhandsofjesus.org for interviews or if the comments of this book have helped you.

Email: extendedhandsofjesus@yahoo.com

Edited by Joyce Standish of Las Vegas, Nevada
Cover Design by Hannah Stewart

This book is dedicated to

Father God,

His Son Jesus Christ,

and

The Holy Spirit

Overpowering Influence
of the
Truth

God's Powerful Plan for Your Life

Edward Franklin Eberly

Contents

Acknowledgements

I first want to thank the Lord Jesus Christ for directing and enabling me to write this book. He strongly inspired me, as I wrote this book, giving me the words to write and putting all into order. All the Glory goes to Him for every person who may be touched through reading this book; it is truly God's Book.

I give my love and respect to my beautiful wife Sabina, who has always been there for me. She has been and still is the love of my life, who supports me, encourages me, offering instruments of wisdom and strength for me. Without her, I would never have had the relationship with God that I do, and would have never moved forward with the Lord in my life and ministry. Sabina has always been the perfect care-giver—for our family, her parents, and my mother in the last years of their lives. She is truly the woman so aptly described in the Bible's Proverbs 31. We have had 45 years of marriage that we both believe God Ordained in Heaven for us to share our lives and work together in the ministry.

I give my love and respect to our children, grandchildren, and great-grandchildren. Our children: Troy and his wife Brenda, Trina, Teresa and her husband David, our grandchildren: Brandy, Kyle, Leslie, Shawn, Caitlin, Stephanie, Kelley, Zachary, and Erica Brooke; our great-grandchildren: Aiden, Gabriel,

Jakeb, Carson, Christopher, and our first great-grandaughter Raelynn Marie.

I give a special "thank you" to Madison Houston by whom this book was made possible and to each person who has been an inspiration in sharing with me your help and encouragement in writing this book. I ask God's Blessings for each and every one of you.

Introduction

At the age of 26 I received Jesus Christ as Savior and Lord of my life and have served Him for over 40 years. Being a pastor and an evangelist for many years, this book is based on God's Word and my experiences according to His Word, bringing the promised results into my life.

The purpose of this book is to give you an understanding of God's Truth in His Word in an understandable way that will show you who you are, how you are to act, react, and deal with the many problems you and I face in life today. It is my heart's desire to teach people the things of God that will save them a lot of grief, and they will learn of the pitfalls, and live their lives for God without unnecessary hardships, be blessed, fruitful, and mighty servants of the Lord.

The Bible tells us that God's people are destroyed because of their lack of knowledge

My people are destroyed for lack of knowledge: because thou has rejected knowledge, I will also reject thee, that thou shalt be no priest to me: seeing thou hast forgotten the law of thy God, I will also forget thy children.

(Hosea 4:6)

People are looking for answers, and the only answer is Jesus Christ and His Word to us. I have applied God's Word in my personal life as well as in my ministry and wish to convey to you what I have learned and found to work effectively to please the Lord.

My great concern is about Christians who have little understanding of God's truth. Even though having been born again for many years, they are ill-equipped in their own lives and are not profitable to minister and share the gospel of Jesus Christ to others. It is my desire to see the Body of Christ strong in their personal lives and living an abundant life Jesus Christ purchased for us, and bearing much fruit in their lives by lifting up Jesus by their lifestyle as well as their words. Many times it is because of pastors not properly instructing their flock in the Word of God that we have so many casualties in the church. My desire is to instruct pastors in God's truth that they can properly lead their people to an abundant and fruitful life in Jesus Christ.

This book will help you have a better understanding of God's Word that will bring results in your life. Christianity is a personal relationship with Jesus Christ and not a religion. It is practical and needful in this life as well as going to Heaven, when you leave this earth. Many times people have just considered it for Heaven only, which is the most important thing. But Jesus came to give us life on this earth, a life that is abundant in all things not just a simple humdrum, dull, meaningless, and routine life while here on earth.

God has a plan and purpose for your life and it is my desire that this book will help you find it. We need answers, while we are here on earth. From this book I pray that many of your questions will be answered.

Edward Franklin Eberly

Edward Franklin Eberly

For God so loved the world that he gave his only begotten Son, that whosoever believeth in him should not perish, but have everlasting life. For God sent not his Son into the world to condemn the world; but that the world through him might be saved.
John 3:16-17

1

Salvation

"Yeshua" is the Hebrew word for 'Salvation' commonly replaced with "Jesus," which is a Greek form of the Messiah's name. "And you shall call Him Salvation,'" means to save, to be safe, receive deliverance, aid, health, help, victory, prosperity, and is the term used in the Christian Faith, as many people relate to as being born-again, saved, receiving Jesus Christ as your Lord and Savior and being forgiven for your sins.

For all have sinned, and come short of the glory of God; (Romans 3:23)

This is true, and definitely the most important thing, having your name written in the Lamb's Book of Life.

And whosoever was not found in the book of life was cast into the lake of fire.

(Revelation 20:15)

But in totality Salvation is wholeness of your spirit, soul and body, for which Jesus Christ provided by the shedding of His blood, death, burial and resurrection for those who believe this in their hearts and confess Him as their Lord and Savior with their mouths.

God's plan of Salvation for man is to redeem him and bring him back to Himself. Man will be free from sin and all bondage in his spirit, soul and body and all the evil works of Satan. God knows we will be attacked and tempted by Satan, challenged by the world, and experience wrong desires in our flesh.

So God gave us provision for all that we need pertaining to life and godliness through the knowledge of Jesus Christ that we would be able to overcome anything or need that we would ever have.

According as his divine power hath given unto us all things that pertain unto life and godliness, through the knowledge of him that hath called us to glory and virtue. (2 Peter 1:3)

He has given us power over all evil and evil spirits, making them subject to us. He gave us authority on the earth to be fruitful and multiply. We also are given by God a free will to choose, either doing it God's way or ours.

Notwithstanding in this rejoice not, that the spirits are subject unto you; but rather rejoice, because your names are written in heaven.

(Luke 10:20)

To work out our Salvation with fear and trembling means that we are to be in the fear of Father God in reverence and respect for whom He is and what He has done for us, as we work out the things that are freely given to us, and use them in the ways that are pleasing to Him.

14

Wherefore, my beloved, as ye have always obeyed, not as in my presence only, but now much more in my absence, work out your own salvation with fear and trembling.

(Philippians 2:12)

God gave us the Holy Spirit as our comforter, leader, teacher, and enabler to accomplish what His Word has instructed for us to receive, be and do.

Then he answered and spake unto me, saying, This is the word of the Lord unto Zerubbabel, saying, Not by might, nor by power, but by my spirit, saith the Lord of hosts.

(Zechariah 4:6)

It is not in our strength, but in the power of God, "Not by power, or by might, but by My Spirit saith the Lord." Everything God tells us in His Word we are, we can have, we can be, and what we can do, if we believe it, because by our believing and releasing our faith in His Word activates His power to perform anything according to His Word to us.

We are given the choice of receiving God's plan of Salvation for us that He sent to us Jesus Christ, His only Begotten Son to the Earth as an example in living our lives on this earth to please Him and to purchase the Salvation plan for us that for which He paid by His own blood. If we receive God's plan for us, then we can live a victorious, overcoming, joyful, prosperous, fruitful and productive life. If we reject God's plan, then automatically we accept Satan's plan for us—to hurt and destroy us, and ultimately spend our eternity in the Lake of Fire, separated from God and His followers in heaven forever and all eternity.

That if thou shalt confess with thy mouth the Lord Jesus, and shalt believe in thine heart that God hath raised him from the dead, thou shalt be saved. For with the heart man believeth unto righteousness; and with the mouth confession is made unto salvation. (Romans 10:9-10)

To be born-again and make Jesus Christ our Lord and Savior, we must first believe that Jesus shed His blood, died, was buried, and arose from the dead. Second, ask Jesus to forgive our sins and come into our lives and be the Savior and Lord of our lives. We must mean these beliefs in our hearts, for God knows what is really in our hearts.

For whosoever shall call upon the name of the Lord shall be saved. (Romans 10:13)

2

Water Baptism

You should know that there is no saving merit in water baptism; it will not save you. The time that you should be baptized is following your salvation in Jesus Christ. Babies should never be baptized, but should be dedicated to the Lord until the age of accountability. Only people that know what they did, when they received Jesus Christ as Lord and Savior, should be baptized in water. I have seen and known people that were saved at the age of four, and as adults they remembered it, and it was real to them. There is no set age for people to accept Christ; it is only that they should understand what happened when they received salvation.

In obedience to the Great Commission that our Lord Jesus Christ commanded unto us, we need to be water-baptized.

Go ye therefore, and teach all nations, baptizing them in the name of the Father, and of the Son, and of the Holy Ghost. (Matthew 28:19)

Baptism should be our first act of obedience after we receive Jesus Christ as Lord and Savior. First we believe and secondly, we are baptized.

He that believeth and is baptized shall be saved; but he that believeth not shall be damned.
(Mark 16:16)

In Jewish history water-baptism was the final act that separated them from their Jewish faith and family. Baptism should be our first profession of faith after salvation. It is symbolic of an outward expression to show an inward change. The water shows how the blood of Jesus covered and cleansed us from all sin.

In whom we have redemption through his blood, the forgiveness of sins, according to the riches of his grace; (Ephesians 1:7)

I was baptized ten months after I was born again. In many cases people have been saved a while before they are baptized, because sometimes it takes a while for the pastors to have a Baptismal Service for them. The ideal is to have a Baptismal in your church, so that those just getting saved could be baptized immediately after baptism is explained to them.

In being baptized, we are starting our walk with Jesus the right way by being obedient and preparing for a life of obedience to Him. We need to follow very closely the teaching and examples in the Bible, so that we can imitate them in our actions and do things which will bring us not only results and success in our lives but will please our Lord Jesus Christ.

I was really blessed after being baptized. My pastor was holding a Baptism Service that Sunday and asked who wanted to be baptized.

Several of us said yes, and then the pastor came to me privately and said he could not baptize me because I smoked. He said he would baptize me if I promised to quit smoking, and I agreed.

Several of the other men smoked, but at the time the pastor did not know. My life was up and down like a see-saw. I was saved for ten months but just could not get the victory in my life. I was saved but not spiritually victorious.

I was heavily involved in Martial Arts. This interest was always on my mind, as I worked out different moves and techniques. You could say that involvement was my god, so I had my priorities out of order.

Before the Baptismal Service that afternoon I told my wife that I was going to quit smoking and serve God. But in truth I could not see how in the world I would be able to accomplish this goal. I said, "Lord, I want to serve You and give You my all. Now please give me the power to live for You."

Keep in mind that I knew absolutely nothing about the Bible or Pentecost. I just expressed my desperate cry and need before the Lord. The Baptismal Service was wonderful, I gave my testimony that I had quit smoking and would live my life for Jesus. After the service I really felt good in my spirit, knowing that I had pleased the Lord.

That evening my favorite television show, "Bonanza," came on. I told my wife that I had no desire to watch it, and that I was going to the bedroom to read my Bible and pray. I had never before decided not to watch "Bonanza". She could not believe my choice. When I came out of the bedroom, my wife said that I was glowing. That night changed my life and started me on a journey that is still in progress after over 40 years.

Another thing about water-baptism is the method ministers use to baptize people. Some people are completely immersed in water and some are sprinkled with water. Many say that the importance of baptism is the attitude of your heart, which is true, but not the method, and is clearly defined in the Bible. I believe we should try to do things the way we are taught in the Word of God. Immersion is the way our Lord Jesus was baptized by John the Baptist, and He came straightway out of the water.

And Jesus, when he was baptized, went up straightway out of the water: and, lo, the heavens were opened unto him, and he saw the Spirit of God descending like a dove, and lighting upon him: (Matthew 3:16)

When Philip baptized the eunuch, the Bible states that he and the eunuch came out of the water.

And when they were come up out of the water, the Spirit of the Lord caught away Philip, that the eunuch saw him no more; and he went on his way rejoicing. (Acts 8:39)

These two incidents make it clear that we should be immersed in the water. The blood of Jesus does not cover just part of us but covers all of us. Reflecting on this shows us that we should be covered completely by water.

I realize that some people may have medical issues that would prevent them from being immersed in water. But God knows their hearts, when they can only be sprinkled with water instead of being immersed. But unless immersion is truly impossible, I believe we should follow the example of Jesus and be completely immersed in water.

In this book I am not judging or condemning anyone for anything, but simply making known the way Jesus taught me in His Word and my experiences of walking with Him in the truth.

Some people are baptized yearly because as baptism is like being cleansed spiritually, rededicating yourself, and starting life afresh. It is a wonderful experience to rededicate yourself to the Lord Jesus Christ.

3

The Baptism of the Holy Spirit

The Baptism of the Holy Spirit is the second work of God's grace in our lives following our born-again experience. Baptism of the Holy Spirit is vitally important in our walk with the Lord. It is so important that Jesus told His first followers to tarry, until endued with power from on high.

And, behold, I send the promise of my Father upon you: but tarry ye in the city of Jerusalem, until ye be endued with power from on high.

(Luke 24:49)

Jesus Christ is the one who baptizes us with the Holy Ghost.

And I knew him not: but he that sent me to baptize with water, the same said unto me, Upon whom thou shalt see the Spirit descending, and remaining on him, the same is he which baptizeth with the Holy Ghost. (John 1:33)

There has been much misunderstanding and confusion about this experience, this confusion comes from people asking others if they have received the Holy Ghost, since they believed. The truth is that when persons are born-again,

22

they receive the Holy Spirit into their lives. God's spirit dwells in them, which began when Jesus breathed on His disciples and said, "Receive ye the Holy Ghost."

And when he had said this, he breathed on them and saith unto them, Receive ye the Holy Ghost: (John 20:22)

This baptism is not the Baptism of the Holy Spirit, but the Holy Spirit entering into people to dwell when they are born- again. Jesus told His disciples and other believers not to leave Jerusalem, but to wait for the promise of the Father to be baptized with the Holy Ghost not many days hence. This is the second work of grace in our lives.

And, being assembled together with them, commanded them that they should not depart from Jerusalem, but wait for the promise of the Father, which, saith he, ye have heard of me. For John truly baptized with water; but ye shall be baptized with the Holy Ghost not many days hence. (Acts 1:4-5)

First in our born-again experience, the Holy Spirit comes into us to dwell which confirms that we belong to Christ.

The Spirit itself beareth witness with our spirit, that we are the children of God:
(Romans 8:16)

Secondly, the Holy Spirit empowers us for service.

But ye shall receive power, after that the Holy Ghost is come upon you: and ye shall be witnesses unto me both in Jerusalem, and in all Judea, and in Samaria, and unto the uttermost part of the earth. (Acts 1:8)

When I received the Baptism of the Holy Spirit over 40 years ago, my life was completely changed and took on a different direction. My water-baptism experience, which was on a Sunday afternoon and my Baptism of the Holy Ghost were a continuation of my commitment that same day. I told God that day before my baptism in water that I would quit smoking and live for the Lord, so that the pastor would agree to baptize me. I could not envision how in the world things would work out. My prayer was, "Lord, I quit smoking and I give you my all, now give me the power to live for you." I knew little about the Bible, nothing about Pentecost, Baptism of the Holy Spirit or speaking in tongues.

That evening I went into my bedroom to pray and gave up watching my favorite television program "Bonanza." It was calm and humid with no wind, and the windows were up, as it was a hot summer night. When I went into the bedroom, I was concerned about learning God's Word, and because the Bible was such a huge book I did not see how I could learn it. When I asked God to teach me His Word, all of a sudden the curtains moved back and forth even though there was no wind. The ceiling seemed to light up. Feeling like I was being electrified and I began speaking in an unknown language. I did not know what happened to me because I was lacking in the knowledge of the Bible.

Coming out of the bedroom that night, my wife told me that my countenance was glowing, like me, did not know what had happened, because I looked different. When we went to church that Sunday, the pastor and the congregation also did not know how the change occurred, but noticed a difference in my appearance. They told me that I must have gotten a good dose of salvation.

The church was a Christian Missionary and Alliance Church that did not believe in the Pentecostal experience. One lady there, I believe, understood what had happened to me, but said little to me about it at that time.

Immediately, I saw people and things in a different light. It seemed that my eyes were open to the truth. I was wearing those rose-colored glasses regarding Christians thinking that they were living like the Bible teaches. But then I saw people and situations in the light of the reality of God's Word. I received discernment, even though I did not know much about the Bible. I understood as I read and things really opened up to me. And even more amazing, I felt a hunger for God's Word.

I began to use my faith and see my prayers being answered as never before. I became bold in my faith, and God gave me wisdom in many decisions I made.

As previously mentioned, at that time I was heavily involved in Martial Arts, which God had told me to quit. It was a little difficult to do, but was no real problem because of my love for Jesus Christ and the Word of God. I believe He took my desire for Martial Arts from me so that I could focus on His Word, this focus led to spending up to ten hours a day reading and praying. God gave me a hunger and ability for quoting Scriptures and telling exact chapter and verse where found in the Bible.

It was not until a year later that I knew what experience I had that Sunday evening in June 1971. A friend of mine and fellow-worker at Mack Truck, where I worked, who was a member of the Full Gospel Business Men, told me that I received the Baptism of the Holy Ghost and asked me if I had been using my prayer language. The initial evidence of your receiving the Baptism of the Holy Spirit is speaking in tongues.

And they were all filled with the Holy Ghost, and began to speak with other tongues, as the Spirit gave them utterance. (Acts 2:4)

For they heard them speak with tongues, and magnify God. They answered Peter, (Acts 10:46)

And when Paul had laid his hands upon them, the Holy Ghost came on them; and they spake with tongues, and prophesied. (Acts 19:6)

I told him that I had not spoken in tongues since that night, so he laid hands on me, prayed for me to receive the fluency of my prayer language and instructed me to worship and praise God in my private time and allow what was in my mouth to come forth. I followed his advice, and about one week later started to pray fluently in my prayer language, also called speaking in tongues. Praying in tongues is the perfect prayer of the Holy Ghost praying through you, one that brings forth much of which you are not even aware.

Likewise the Spirit also helpeth our infirmities: for we know not what we should pray for as we ought: but the Spirit itself maketh intercession for us with groanings which cannot be uttered. And he that searcheth the hearts knoweth what is the mind of the Spirit, because he maketh intercession for the saints according to the will of God. (Romans 8:26-27)

We have control, when we want to pray in tongues, just as we do when we pray in our understanding.

And the spirits of the prophets are subject to the prophets. (1 Corinthians 14:32)

Sometimes the Holy Spirit causes us to go from our prayer of understanding into tongues for the purposes of God to be prayed about. As well, when we worship and praise Him, our tongue language will just flow from us. Two ways we are to pray: our understanding and in tongues. Many times when we run out of things to say and want to go deeper into God, we allow the Holy Ghost to pray through us, which is praying in tongues, as I had experienced that long-ago day of my experience of the Holy Spirit; this is complete fulfillment of our prayer lives.

The second misunderstanding and confusion is about the Gift of Tongues. Our prayer language, praying in the Holy Ghost, is explained as follows:

But ye, beloved, building up yourselves on your most holy faith, praying in the Holy Ghost,

(Jude 20)

Have all the gifts of healing? Do all speak with tongues? do all interpret? (1 Corinthians 12: 30)

It is true that not everyone has the Gift of Tongues as stated in the above Scripture, because we are told that not all do speak in

27

tongues. When I speak of the Holy Ghost and Holy Spirit, they are one.

For to one is given by the Spirit the word of wisdom; to another the word of knowledge by the same Spirit; To another faith by the same Spirit; to another the gifts of healing by the same Spirit; To another the working of miracles; to another prophecy; to another discerning of spirits; to another divers kinds of tongues; to another the interpretation of tongues, But all these worketh that one and the selfsame Spirit, dividing to every man severally as he will. (1 Corinthians 12:8-11)

This Scripture speaks of the gift being used in meetings, a church service, or with a group of people in which not everybody does participate in the Gift of Tongues. Nine gifts of the Holy Spirit operate in our lives, as God wills. When this gift is in operation in the church or with a group of people, there must be an interpretation.

Wherefore let him that speaketh in an unknown tongue pray that he may interpret. Else when thou shalt bless with the spirit, how shall he that occupieth the room of the unlearned say Amen at thy giving of thanks, seeing he understandeth not what thou sayest?

(1 Corinthians 14:13,16)

Our prayer language in our personal prayer life has three purposes:

First, we are to magnify, exalt and worship our Lord.

For they heard them speak with tongues, and magnify God. Then answered Peter, (Acts 10:46)

Many times we are not able to put into our own prayer, praise, worship, or our heartfelt love in words that we really mean. Our adoration toward God goes beyond mere words, so we pray and worship the Lord Jesus Christ by praying in the Holy Spirit (tongues).

Second, we build up ourselves, strengthened and encouraged in our spirit man by praying in tongues. Out of our belly shall flow the rivers of living water which is the Holy Ghost coming out of the very core of our being to reach others in the power of Jesus Christ.

But ye, beloved, building up yourselves on your most holy faith, praying in the Holy Ghost,
(Jude 20)

He that believeth on me, as the scripture hath said, out of his belly shall flow rivers of living water. (John 7:38)

Third, many times we do not know how to pray for ourselves and others. Sometimes God will pray through us in tongues for someone we do not even know, for example, missionaries in Africa or anywhere that need God to move in their lives. Many times in my personal life and also my ministry to others, I have prayed in tongues. God immediately or shortly thereafter gave me the result or answer that I needed.

Likewise the Spirit also helpeth our infirmities: for we know not what we should pray for as we ought: but the Spirit itself maketh intercession for us with groanings which cannot be uttered. And he that searcheth the hearts knoweth what is the mind of the Spirit, because he maketh intercession for the saints according to the will of God. (Romans 8:26-27)

One time I needed to know how to hang a fragile display mantle of good size in my living room. I prayed in tongues and God showed me what to use and how to do the task. By the way, the mantle hanging turned out perfectly. I assure you it was not my skill that made it a perfect job.

One time I was praying for a lady who needed deliverance but there was something that was missing. I prayed and nothing happened. I prayed in tongues and God gave me the needed answer. When I told her what God had revealed to me, she was set free.

Many times we do not know how to pray, but the Holy Ghost knows and prays the perfect prayer through us. I was called out to pray for a lady who was sick. When I went to her home, her husband greeted me, when I went into the house. His wife looked like death, so I really needed God's help. So as always, I quietly prayed in tongues in the Spirit and then she and her husband began talking. A difficult conflict between the two of them was obvious. They talked it out and I acted as the mediator not saying or doing very much. Finally, when they forgave each other and got themselves in one accord, she immediately literally glowed. I did not have to pray further because she was healed. She needed not a healing prayer, but reconciliation with her husband. She told me later that she accomplished twice the usual work done the next day. I did not know her need, but God did. So I let the Holy Ghost pray through me to receive the perfect prayer for the perfect answer.

Not all people will have the gift of tongues operating in their lives, as I have explained in this chapter. The prayer language is for all people who are born-again and receive the Baptism of the Holy Spirit with the evidence of speaking in tongues (prayer language). We develop our prayer language by using it like any other gifting that God places in our lives.

We must pray in tongues (prayer language), but not all have the gift of tongues which are two different giftings that God gives to His children.

Satan has fought so hard this command of Jesus Christ to the Church, because he realizes that with this experience we are empowered to defeat him and have victory over him. Satan will try to prevent us from receiving the Baptism of the Holy Spirit so we would not have the power to defeat him. Satan hinders us from walking in the power of God and leaves us powerless. If it was necessary for the first believers to receive this empowerment from on high, by the command of Jesus, I believe it is now even more necessary, as we look around us. We are a continuation of the beginning of the Church of Jesus Christ.

Apostle Paul said he thanked God that he spoke in tongues more than any of the people to which he was speaking in Corinth.

I thank my God, I speak with tongues more than ye all: (1 Corinthians 14:18)

I know what my prayer language has done for me, and believe that it made the difference between success and failure in my life. I conclude that Paul would not have been the Great Man of God who wrote over half of the New Testament or the chief of all the Apostles, if he had not used his prayer language (tongues).

Remember, Jesus commanded them not to depart from Jerusalem until they received the promise of the Holy Ghost. Before we can do God's work, we need to be empowered by God. The Baptism of the Holy Ghost is not an option, but a commandment by Jesus Christ and "a must" for us in order to fulfill in our lives and find success in the plan that God has for us.

And, being assembled together with them, commanded them that they should not depart from Jerusalem, but wait for the promise of the Father, which, saith he, ye have heard of me. For John truly baptized with water; but ye shall be baptized with the Holy Ghost not many days hence. (Acts 1:4-5)

The Baptism of the Holy Spirit empowers us to live a victorious and overcoming life and to be a vessel for our Lord and Savior Jesus Christ.

4

Tithing

The tithe is one-tenth of the annual produce of one's land or one's annual income used to help support a church or ministry. Tithing is God's Financial System for us to provide for the preaching of the Gospel of Jesus Christ to the whole world. The Great Commission of Jesus is to baptize all in the name of the Father, Son, and of the Holy Ghost and teach all nations everything that He has commanded us.

Go ye therefore, and teach all nations, baptizing them in the name of the Father, and of the Son, and of the Holy Ghost. Teaching them to observe all things whatsoever I have commanded you: and, lo, I am with you always, even unto the end of the world. (Matthew 28:19-20)

Tithes and offerings are God's way to provide for the spreading of the Gospel, as well as blessing us and meeting our financial needs.

But thou shalt remember the Lord thy God: for it is he that giveth thee power to get wealth that he may establish his covenant which he sware unto thy fathers, as it is this day.

(Deuteronomy 8:18)

Everything we give above the tithe (one tenth of our income) is considered an offering. Generally our local church should receive our tithe, because that is where we are fed. We can also give offerings there, or any ministry or people that has a need to which God directs us to give.

God cannot bless us financially, if we do not tithe, for if we do not sow, neither will we reap.

Be not deceived; God is not mocked: for whatsoever a man soweth, that shall he also reap. (Galatians 6:7)

Abraham first paid tithe to Melchisedec who was a type of Christ.

For this Melchisedec, king of Salem, priest of the most high God, who met Abraham returning from the slaughter of the kings, and blessed him; To whom also Abraham gave a tenth part of all; first being by interpretation King of righteousness, and after that also King of Salem, which is, King of peace; (Hebrews 7:1-2)

Tithing began before the law and is carried on through, as Jesus advised us not to leave tithing undone.

Woe unto you, scribes and Pharisees, hypocrites! for ye pay tithe of mint and anise and cummin, and have omitted the weightier matters of the law, judgment, mercy, and faith; these ought ye to have done, and not to leave the other undone. (Matthew 23:23)

God's Word tells us that we are robbing God, if we do not give the tithe, and it is also the only time in God's Word that He tells us to prove Him.

Will a man rob God? Yet ye have robbed me. But ye say, Wherein have we robbed thee? In tithes and offerings. Ye are cursed with a curse: for ye have robbed me, even this whole nation. Bring ye all the tithes into the storehouse, that there may be meat in mine house, and prove me now herewith, saith the Lord of hosts, if I will not open you the windows of heaven, and pour you out a blessing, that there shall not be room enough to receive it. (Malachi 3:8-10)

Remember, the purpose for tithes and offerings is to spread the Gospel of Jesus Christ to everyone on this earth and to secure your financial needs and future.

For the person who tithes three promises are given: The windows of heaven will be open for us, and there will not be room enough to receive it. He will rebuke Satan for our sakes, that He will not destroy our fruits of the ground or our vine cast its fruit before the time in the field. These promises meaning protection of our income and jobs as well as of our material things; also we will be called Blessed. For our offerings God said that if we give, it will be given to us in good measure pressed down, shaken and running over; men will give to us. The same measure that we give shall be again returned to us.

Give, and it shall be given unto you; good measure, pressed down, and shaken together, and running over, shall men give into your bosom. For with the same measure that ye mete withal it shall be measured to you again. (Luke 6:38)

I first started to tithe shortly after being saved. God spoke to my heart about tithing at the worst time in my life. I was laid off work, my unemployment money ran out, and I was on welfare, drawing $85 weekly plus food stamps. Additionally, my wife and I had three small children at that time. I said, "Lord, my expenses and food total to $125 weekly to make it, and you want me to tithe leaving me with about $76.50? I gave in and thought: I'm not making it on $85.00 much less to make it with $76.50. I turned it over to the Lord and obeyed Him even though to me it was impossible. But I recalled the Bible's Scriptures.

But Jesus beheld them, and said unto them, With men this is impossible; but with God all things are possible. (Matthew 19:26)

For approximately five and a half months God stretched our money, so that we did not miss one bill payment, we ate very well and also lived better than we had while I was working. God brought money to me from many different people and in many different ways. One time I was called by a radio station program called, "What Do You Know," where they randomly called townspeople and asked them a question to which the answer was posted at various business places. My mother had given me the answer a short time before. I knew the answer, that morning while washing the dishes, I told my wife that I was going to get called on the next call; I just knew it. About two minutes later they called and that day I became $144 richer, which for me was a lot of money at that time. Through trusting the Lord and His Word, I was blessed in an impossible situation for nearly six months.

I wish to go on record saying that some people claim they cannot afford to tithe, but the truth is they cannot afford not to. There is no situation in which we are in that we cannot give the tithe, even if we only have a dime, we then give a penny. We get ourselves out of debt by tithing and giving offerings, not hoarding our money. Remember the widow with the two mites? She put into the treasury the two mites and Jesus said that she gave more than anyone there.

And there came a certain poor widow, and she threw in two mites, which make a farthing. And he called unto him his disciples, and saith unto them, Verily I say unto you, That this poor widow hath cast more in than all they which have cast into the treasury: For all they did cast in of their abundance; but she of her want did cast in all that she had, even all her living. (Mark 12:42-44)

Rich people put much money into the treasury but in the eyes of Jesus, He measures what we give proportionately to what we have. For example, if a man has $1,000,000 and gives $50,000 and another man has $100 and gives $50, who gave the most in God's eyes? The answer is that the man with the $100 gave 50% and the man with the $1,000,000 gave 5%. The world would value the biggest amount given, but God looks at what we have proportionately to what we give. The widow actually gave all 100%.

God spoke to me about another question concerning what I am to tithe on my gross income or net pay. One evening I was preparing myself for a speaking engagement, and God told me that I was supposed to tithe from my gross income not my net pay. Until that time I had been tithing on my net pay, so I told God that starting from my next paycheck, I would tithe on my gross pay. That word was given to me on a Sunday evening. At that time for a little over a year my wife and I were trying to sell our home with no success. I just could not seem to find a buyer for my home. Three days later on a Wednesday, even before I got my next paycheck to pay my tithe... guess what? Our home was sold. That was an amazing sale, as we got a good price for it. Also the Buyers got a good deal, so everyone made out well on that transaction. Does that not sound like God?

When we obey Him, things happen in our lives. However, many times things are held up in our lives because of disobedience or because God is trying to show us something. In tithing the government takes their share off our gross amount, and then we get our net pay. If the government takes their money off the top of our pay, then God, who is more important than the government, should also get His share off the top.

Our money represents our labor and the giving of ourselves of something that is of necessity for us to live in this world. When we take this step, then we are preparing ourselves for God to bless us and meet all of our needs. God tells us that he will supply all of our needs according to His riches in glory by Christ Jesus.

But my God shall supply all your need according to his riches in glory by Christ Jesus.
(Philippians 4:19)

Many Christians believe the above Scripture, but if we do not tithe, we cannot claim it. There are conditions to be met with all of God's promises to us. We are told by Apostle Paul that the church at Philippi was the only church that supported him, when he left Macedonia, which qualified them to receive, because they gave their tithes and offerings.

Notwithstanding ye have well done, that ye did communicate with my affliction... Not because I desire a gift; but I desire fruit that may abound to your account. (Philippians 4:14,17)

Therefore the Holy Spirit spoke the words that "My God shall supply all your needs according to His riches in glory by Christ Jesus" to the Philippians. Always remember, you cannot out-give God.

Most times when we talk about tithing and giving, the subject regards only our substance and money, but, in truth, it goes beyond that. We spend at least 40 hours or more weekly on our jobs to earn a living out of a 168-hour week which is nearly 25% of our week. God not only wants us to give our money, but our attention and time to Him and His work for us. If we tithe our week to Him, it would be 16.8 hours per week, or 2 hours and 24 minutes daily, about the length of time for us to watch a movie. We think nothing of looking at television 4 or 5 hours a day.

I am not advising you to daily keep a tab on your time. But daily you could easily set time aside for the things of God by prayer, reading, ministering to others, and doing for others. Another thing is to be on time, when you make a commitment to be there at a certain time; if you do not, you are stealing that person's time that you make wait for you. One example is that if church starts at 11: 00 a.m., be there a little before, but do not come in at 11:30 a.m. To be late, you disrupt the service and being tardy does not show respect to God or your fellow-members.

If you, regularly arrive at work on time, but constantly are late for church, you are showing God that your job is more important to you than He is. I know that sometimes being late is unavoidable, but if possible notify the people involved. Continue to go to church, even if you are late in unavoidable situations. I am not speaking to people who at times are late because of unavoidable situations, but to those who make a practice of lateness, and to those who make no effort to be on time for most of their commitments.

God wants you to prosper and be in good health, as your soul prospers meaning as you grow spiritually by God's Word, and you will have faith, and believe it and receive His promises for your life. He gives you power to get wealth to establish His covenant.

But thou shalt remember the Lord thy God: for it is he that giveth thee power to get wealth that he may establish his covenant which he sware unto thy fathers, as it is this day.

(Deuteronomy 8:18)

God wants us to have abundance.

And the Lord shall make thee plenteous in goods, in the fruit of thy body, and in the fruit of thy cattle, and in the fruit of thy ground, in the land which the Lord sware unto thy fathers to give thee. (Deuteronomy 28:11)

God even tells us that He will bless us, our storehouses, and all in life that we set out to accomplish.

The Lord shall command the blessing upon thee in thy storehouses, and in all that thou settest thine hand unto; and he shall bless thee in the land which the Lord thy God giveth thee.

(Deuteronomy 28:8)

God wants you to give Him your heart and show your obedience, so that He can prosper you in all ways.

In closing Chapter 4, the bottom line is that we are to be conduits or good stewards through whom God can funnel money to help others and get out the Gospel. We have tremendous needs in people and ministries around us, so we should not lavish ourselves, but use our understanding as a way to show the love of God to people and spread His Word to the world. Our desire should be to be prosperous and enjoy an abundant and fruitful life. We need to seek the face of God about who we give to, how much, and when He wants us to give to others. I am speaking about our giving above the tithe. So in closing, just have a giving heart willing to give as God directs.

5

Faith

The foundation of the Christian faith is that we first believe God exists and that He will always reward those who truly diligently seek Him.

But without faith it is impossible to please him; for he that cometh to God must believe that he is, and that he is a rewarder of them that diligently seek him. (Hebrews 11:6)

Our faith must only be anchored in God and His Word (Covenant) to us by His Son Jesus Christ, who by His Blood paid for our Salvation. This Covenant was given to us for the forgiveness of sins and provides a home in Heaven when we leave our human bodies. But in this life Jesus has given us everything pertaining to this life and godliness, so that we can live a prosperous and fruitful life while on this earth.

According as his divine power hath given unto us all things that pertain unto life and godliness, through the knowledge of him that hath called us to glory and virtue. (2 Peter 1-3)

Faith is the title deed of things believed for and the evidence of things not seen.

NOW faith is the substance of things hoped for, the evidence of things not seen.

(Hebrews 11:1)

We are also told that without faith, it is impossible to please God. If we do not have faith, God will not be pleased with us.

But without faith it is impossible to please him; for he that cometh to God must believe that he is, and that he is a rewarder of them that diligently seek him. (Hebrews 11:6)

Faith is simply putting our trust in God's Word and His Promises to us, and to believe that they will manifest in our lives.

It is better to trust in the Lord than to put confidence in man. (Psalms 118:8)

When we really have faith in any of God's Promises to us, we will have peace about it; we will not worry, or be afraid to take risks, which really are not risks when we step out in faith in God's Word, for we expect God's Word to do what it says it will do.

The Bible tells us that faith comes to us by hearing and also hearing by God's Word.

So then faith cometh by hearing, and hearing by the word of God. (Romans 10:17)

God's Word is our spiritual food. We need to continue hearing just as our physical bodies need to keep eating continually proper food to keep healthy. Feeding our spirit with God's Word causes our faith to be built up. We need to hear it taught and preached and also read the Bible for ourselves to clearly hear and build up our faith. A good way to read the Bible is out loud, for there is a creative force that we speak which benefits us more than just quiet reading. We must pray and meditate on what we read to gain understanding and revelation of the Biblical words. God spoke the world into existence, when He said: "Let there be Light."

And God said, Let there be light: and there was light. (Genesis 1:3)

Thus, a creative power exists in our speaking out loud. Light travels at 186,000 miles a second. When God commanded "Light Be," at that rate which is 669,600,000 miles an hour, everything expanded. For example: Imagine everything is dark, and then the light penetrates the darkness and spreads in all directions at nearly 670 million miles an hour for the past thousands of years. This light will continue to expand at that rate for all eternity. We cannot begin to imagine how large the universe is. Honestly, I cannot comprehend these figures. This understanding is beyond human ability and is a God 'thing", that gives us a small idea of how huge the world around us is and how big and almighty our Father God really is, as the hymn says, "How Great Thou Art."

We can get enough food for our physical bodies and should not overeat, but we can never get enough spiritual food from God's Word. We need to feed and meditate on His Word. Such deep thinking will make our faith more knowledgeable and stronger. We also will live a better life and be more productive for Jesus. If our minds are on worldly things—TV programs, sports, computer games—that will become first place in our lives. There is nothing wrong with good TV programs, sports, or many things that we do, but our priorities need to be in Divine Order, first things first. God's Word will only come out of us in time of need by the Holy Spirit, taken from what we have put into our spirit by reading and meditating. Nothing in, nothing out.

Faith is always expressed in the present tense, while Hope is in the future. For example: When we believe and receive healing for our bodies, as soon as we release our faith into the spirit world, it begins, whether manifesting in our body immediately or not. Some healings are instant and others are gradual, but in reality our healing begins immediately after releasing our faith. Our going to Heaven is our Hope, because we will not go there until Jesus comes for us or we die. That is the future, so that is our Hope. We must always consider anything for which we use our faith must be done NOW in the Present Tense or otherwise, we will not receive it. Faith says I have it NOW.

Therefore I say unto you, What things soever ye desire, when ye pray, believe that ye receive them, and ye shall have them. (Mark 11:24)

There are conditions that we must meet in using our faith, so that we will receive the results we requested. First, a clean heart free from sin and disobedience towards God, or otherwise, our heart will condemn us and we would have no confidence in our receiving from the Lord.

Beloved, if our heart condemn us not, then have we confidence toward God. And whatsoever we ask, we receive of him, because we keep his commandments, and do those things that are pleasing in his sight. (1 John 3:21-22)

We also cannot have any unforgiveness in our heart toward anyone including ourselves and God's love in our heart.

And when ye stand praying, forgive, if ye have aught against any: that your Father also which is in heaven may forgive you your trespasses. But if ye do not forgive, neither will your Father which is in heaven forgive your trespasses.

(Mark 11:25-26)

For in Jesus Christ neither circumcision availeth any thing, nor uncircumcision; but faith which worketh by love. (Galatians 5:6)

When our hearts are right we find the scripture or scriptures that apply to our need, for example like healing and claim it by faith that we have the result NOW, present tense. Faith is always in the NOW, whether it affects us immediately or not, it began when we released our faith. We determine to stand until faith affects or improves our lives.

Therefore I say unto you, What things soever ye desire, when ye pray, believe that ye receive them, and ye shall have them. (Mark 11:24)

You must be careful of the words you speak, and use only faith words. You must not use words like: Where is my healing? Or maybe I did not receive my healing. Keep confessing out loud God's Word regarding healing, and praising God for your healing. You must act as if you are healed and do something that you could not do before and see yourself healed. If someone asks, "Are you healed?" tell them "By Jesus stripes I am healed," and remember to be positive.

Who his own self bare our sins in his own body on the tree, that we, being dead to sins, should live unto righteousness: by whose stripes ye were healed. (1 Peter 2:24)

This Scripture cites instances where Satan steals people's faith that they do not receive, by forcing them to be negative and to confess negative words. The power of the tongue holds in its grasp both Death and Life.

Death and life are in the power of the tongue: and they that love it shall eat the fruit thereof.

(Proverbs 18:21)

Our words justify us, and by these words we are condemned.

For by thy words thou shall be justified, and by thy words thou shalt be condemned.

(Matthew 12:37)

If we do not receive instant signs of our healing, we must be patient, which in reality is faith's twin. After following the will of God, we must show patience to be rewarded by receiving the promise.

Cast not away therefore your confidence, which hath great recompence of reward. For ye have need of patience, that, after ye have done the will of God, ye might receive the promise.

(Hebrews 10:35-36)

Patience is a force that if we use it and stand our ground, we will be mature and our lives will lack nothing of merit.

But let patience have her perfect work, that ye may be perfect and entire, wanting nothing.

(James 1:4)

Our faith is our most vital possession, one that is as critical to our spiritual life as to our physical life as air is to our human bodies. Without air, we would die in a few minutes. Without faith, we would be disconnected from God forever, because God's power and our faith lead to salvation.

Who are kept by the power of God through faith unto salvation ready to be revealed in the last time. (1Peter 1:5)

For example: Using a rope to represent faith, imagine that you are drowning in a lake and someone throws you a rope. You take hold of it, and that person starts pulling you out of the water. In your rescue you are connected to your rescuer by a rope. Of course, if you no longer hold onto the rope, you are disconnected from that person and you will drown. If you depart from your faith in Jesus Christ, you will be disconnected from God.

And you, that were sometime alienated and enemies in your mind by wicked works, yet now hath he reconciled. In the body of his flesh through death, to present you holy and unblameable and unreproveable in his sight: If ye continue in the faith grounded and settled, and be not moved away from the hope of the gospel, which ye have heard, and which was preached to every creature which is under heaven; whereof I Paul am made a minister; (Colossians 1: 21-23)

We must also continue in the faith, until we depart from this life.

Every born-again child of God has been given the measure of faith.

For I say, through the grace given unto me, to every man that is among you, not to think of himself more highly than he ought to think; but to think soberly, according as God hath dealt to every man the measure of faith. (Romans 12:3)

We all receive the same portion of faith, but it is up to us how much that faith will grow and how strong it will become. Faith comes by hearing God's Word and grows. We exercise faith by claiming God's Word for ourselves and to minister to others until the promise of God becomes a reality to us. To have strong bodies, we need to use barbells and weights what some refer to as "resistance" to strengthen our muscles. Our faith and spirit-man resistance or opposition causes us to grow and become stronger, but only if we remain steadfast in our faith in whatever we believe until it manifests in our lives.

When you receive by faith, you confess that you have it and you act like you have it, but in reality your condition may become worse. Instead of giving up, you choose to stand. Remember after you have done all, stand firmly for your God given rights.

If you stand for your rights until the healing is a reality, and refuse to give up, not only will your faith grow, but you will be strengthened. Your stand is not always pleasant or easy. If you desire to become strong and mighty in the faith, you will have to "stretch" it and stand, no matter what. Spiritual pain in building your spirit-man is like physical pain in building your body. This effort recalls an old adage: "No pain, No gain," and that is reality in your spiritual walk with Jesus. Male believers need to man-up and women believers need to woman-up to this truth instead of acting like babies, whimpering when they are tried and tested. In truth, your trials and tests will make you bitter or better, your choice. God hears a sinner's prayer for repentance, but He does not hear sinners when they pray out of His will for their lives. God clearly hears the obedient Christian who worships Him and does His will.

Now we know that God heareth not sinners: but if any man be a worshipper of God, and doeth his will, him he heareth. (John 9:31)

If I regard iniquity in my heart, the Lord will not hear me: (Psalms 66:18)

Remember whatsoever we ask of Him, we receive of Him, because we keep His commandments and do those things that are pleasing in His sight. By keeping His commandments, we believe in the name of His Son Jesus Christ, and love one another, and live a life pleasing to the Lord while walking in obedience to Him.

And whatsoever we ask, we receive of him, because we keep his commandments, and do those things that are pleasing in his sight. And this is his commandment, That we should believe on the name of his Son Jesus Christ, and love one another, as he gave us commandment.

(1 John 3:22-23)

According to His word, being confident that if anything you ask is according to His Word, He hears you. He hears you no matter what you ask, and you know that He will grant your requests.

And this is the confidence that we have in him, that, if we ask any thing according to his will, he heareth us: And if we know that he hear us, whatsoever we ask, we know that we have the petitions that we desired of him.

(1 John 5:14-15)

God's Promises are for His Children who are living for Jesus Christ, because all the Promises for this life and for all eternity are in Jesus Christ. We do not "earn" the promises of God, as they are all by God's grace. We must realize that there are conditions to God's Promises to us.

In conclusion, our faith simply believes what God says in His Word to us, acting by applying it to our lives. We must believe, speak, and act as if we already have our request, not allowing our circumstances or situations or any influence on this earth to take us away from what we are standing in faith for. God has certain conditions for His promises to us: Each of us must have both a pure heart and faith, until giving us our promises. It is an accepted fact that true faith will bring peace to us and guarantees results.

6

Unforgiveness

Unforgiveness is one of the most common sins of which all humanity, including many in the Body of Christ, are guilty. Often, even true Christians, will overlook the importance of forgiving others; in the eyes of God it is a very serious offence. Jesus said to forgive. When praying, if we have anything against anyone we must forgive them so Father God will forgive our trespasses. However, if we do not forgive, our Father in Heaven will not forgive us.

And when ye stand praying, forgive, if ye have aught against any: that your Father also which is in heaven may forgive you your trespasses. But if ye do not forgive, neither will your Father which is in heaven forgive your trespasses.

(Mark 11:25-26)

Notice that these two verses follow the faith and mountain-moving verses which show the Power of God will be stopped in our lives, and we still must live with sins, if we harbor unforgiveness in our hearts against anyone.

For verily I say unto you, That whosoever shall say unto this mountain, Be thou removed and be thou cast into the sea; and shall not doubt in his heart, but shall believe that those things which he saith shall come to pass; he shall have whatsoever he saith. Therefore I say unto you, What things soever ye desire when ye pray, believe that ye receive them, and ye shall have them. (Mark 11:23-24)

The most extreme case that can be found is in the Bible. A king was taking account of his servants who owed him money; one owed him 10,000 talents (if silver $52,800,000). The king commanded that he, his wife, children and all their worldly goods would be sold, until the debt was paid. The servant fell down and worshipped the king saying, "Lord, have patience with me and I will pay thee." The lord, indeed, had compassion on him, forgave him the debt, and freed the man. This same servant found a servant who owed him a hundred pence ($44.00). His servant begged for patience, but the servant denied him any patience and cast him into prison until he paid the debt. The fellow-servants saw this and told their lord of all this unfairness. The lord of the servant called him back and said, "Thou wicked servant, I forgave you of all that debt because you asked me. Should you not have compassion on your fellow-servant as I had pity on thee?" Angry, the lord delivered him to the tormentors, until he paid all due to him. Jesus summed up this example by saying, "So likewise shall my Heavenly Father do also unto you, if you from your hearts forgive not every one of his brother's trespasses."

Therefore is the kingdom of heaven likened unto a certain king, which would take account of his servants. And when he had begun to reckon, one was brought unto him, which owed him ten thousand talents. But forasmuch as he had not to pay, his lord commanded him to be sold, and his wife, and children, and all that he had, and payment to be made. The servant therefore fell down, and worshipped him, saying, Lord, have patience with me, and I will pay thee all. Then the lord of that servant was moved with compassion, and loosed him, and forgave him the debt. But the same servant went out, and found one of his fellow-servants, which owed him an hundred pence: and he laid hands on him, and took him by the throat, saying, Pay me that thou owest. And his fellow-servant fell down at his feet, and besought him, saying, Have patience with me, and I will pay thee all. And he would not: but went and cast him into prison, till he should pay the debt. So when his fellow-servants saw what was done, they were very sorry, and came and told unto their lord all that was done. Then his lord, after that he had called him, said unto him, O thou wicked servant, I forgave thee all that debt, because thou desiredst me: Shouldest not thou also have had compassion on thy fellow-servant, even as I had pity on thee? And his lord was wroth, and delivered him to the tormentors, till he should pay all that was due unto him. So likewise shall my heavenly Father do also unto you, if ye from your hearts forgive not every one his brother their trespasses.

(Matthew 18:23-35)

The revelation from these scriptures is: The first servant received forgiveness of his great debt of over $52 million dollars, and then his servant owed him $44 dollars, and would not forgive him. Being forgiven for millions of dollars appears to be somewhat ridiculous, then not forgiving another for a few dollars. In God's eyes we have been forgiven for much.

As a personal example, I have been forgiven for much in my life. If someone offends me in some way and I choose not to forgive them, then in God's eyes my behavior appears ridiculous, as the money that was not forgiven by the servant. If we know Jesus Christ as our Lord and Savior we have all been forgiven for much, so we need to have the same spirit and attitude toward that person or persons as God has toward us—"A forgiving God." When we see things as they really are, stop and think, then we can see the God-like way to go is to walk in love and forgiveness toward everyone.

To not forgive, we break our fellowship with God and retain our sins. If we do not forgive, from the point that we choose unforgiveness toward others, we will no longer be forgiven by God. In unforgiveness, there is bondage and we are easily held captive and tormented in our mind. Testimonies of women who were raped and did not forgive the person or persons involved are quite common. Such women freely admitted to having had nightmares and all types of torment, until they forgave and received God's peace.

When we forgive, we are turning over the person and situation to God to deal with the situation, as it is, then out of our hands and into His. Then we can effectively pray for such violators to receive Jesus as Lord and Savior and be delivered from the demon forces that have them in captivity and be set free. People who forgive and pray for the one that violated them have powerful prayer power that brings effective results for the violator. These are prayers for others, especially when we are hurt by someone and turn them over to God in prayer. They are special to Him, for we are showing mercy toward them, and God will answer in a mighty way.

Whether we forgive a person or not does not affect them, but if we do not forgive them it does affect us, as forgiveness is for our benefit not theirs. In our life time, many people and situations come into our lives. If we are Christians, Satan tries to cause friction by forcing us to get into holding a grudge state of mind. We must make a quality decision not to hold a grudge and forgive all, as the occasion arises. It is inevitable that we will be challenged by the opportunity to hold unforgiveness toward someone, but we must not let harmful unforgiveness become a part of our lives.

The best way to deal with unforgiveness is that when someone transgresses against you or wrongs you, immediately say, "Lord I forgive _____ for _____." You do not say these words because you feel like forgiving, but it is a decision of your will in spite of your feelings, because your Heavenly Father commanded you to forgive. You might feel like hitting the aggressor or feel angry. But say the above-noted words, and ask God to help us love them and then immediately pray for them and do so daily. You will find that when you are praying for someone, you cannot hold a grudge or unforgiveness. Your feelings will eventually change toward them. Satan will try to bring back to your mind the wrong done to you, but you should command him to go in the name of Jesus Christ and say, "I have forgiven _____." End of story.

Following are a few concise suggestions pertaining to violations:

- Tell God that you forgive the person for their violation.
- Ask God to help you love this person.
- Pray daily for God to help the person.
- Be aware of how your attitude will eventually change toward the person.

7

Healing

One of the names for God in the Bible is "Jehovah Rophi," the Lord who heals you. God sent His Word to heal us and deliver us from being destroyed.

He sent his word, and healed them, and delivered them from their destructions.

(Psalms 107:20)

God's Word is medicine to our bodies that works with no side effects. Just as a doctor prescribes and directs a patient to take medicine for an illness, God gives us His Word to instruct us how to receive healing for our bodies. We believe and receive our healing by faith. When it does not manifest immediately, we continue to stand in faith and patience and confess with our mouths that we are healed until healing manifests in our bodies.

My son, attend to my words; incline thine ear unto my sayings. Let them not depart from thine eyes; keep them in the midst of thine heart. For they are life unto those that find them, and health to all their flesh. (Proverbs 4:20-22)

Therefore I say unto you, What things soever ye desire, when ye pray, believe that ye receive them, and ye shall have them. (Mark 11:24)

Sickness and disease are curses to mankind. We should all remember that Jesus Christ saved us from the Curse of the Law.

Christ hath redeemed us from the curse of the law, being made a curse for us: for it is written, Cursed is every one that hangeth on a tree:
(Galatians 3:13)

The 39 stripes that Jesus bore on His back represents the 39 types of diseases He bore for us, so that we could be free from sickness and disease. Jesus took it all on Himself, so that we could be healed and live a healthy life for Him.

But he was wounded for our transgressions, he was bruised for our iniquities: the chastisement of our peace was upon him; and with his stripes we are healed. (Isaiah 53:5)

God desires that as our soul prospers, so shall we prosper and be in health

Beloved, I wish above all things that thou mayest prosper and be in health, even as thy soul prospereth. (3 John 2)

This means as we prosper in our knowledge and understanding of God's Word, we get the revelation of the promises Jesus gave us. Our salvation that Jesus Christ paid for gave us not only a home in Heaven when we leave this earth, but everything that pertains to life and godliness.

According as his divine power hath given unto us all things that pertain unto life and godliness, through the knowledge of him that hath called us to glory and virtue: (2 Peter 1:3)

God also tells us that He forgives all our sins and wickedness and promises to heal all our diseases.

Who forgiveth all thine iniquities; who healeth all thy diseases; (Psalms 103:3)

As previously stated, sickness is a curse, Christ redeemed us from this curse (all born-again Christians). Thus, healing is a promise to us from Jesus Christ; it is an all-important part of our Salvation.

Christ hath redeemed us from the curse of the law, being made a curse for us: for it is written, Cursed is every one that hangeth on a tree:

(Galatians 3:13)

Our bodies are the temple of the Holy Ghost.

What? Know ye not that your body is the temple of the Holy Ghost which is in you, which ye have of God, and ye are not your own?

(1 Corinthians 6:19)

God wants us to take care of our bodies. Many ways exist for sickness and disease to come into our bodies. Worry and stress, fear, lack of sleep, improper diet, lack of exercise and overworking will not give us enough rest. Not dressing warmly in the extreme cold. Other times a direct attack of Satan will occur. We all should think deeply about the woman in the Bible who was bent over for 18 years because Satan had her bound in that manner as punishment.

And ought not this woman, being a daughter of Abraham, whom Satan hath bound, lo, these eighteen years, be loosed from this bond on the Sabbath day? (Luke 13:16)

An epidemic of people passing on germs of the flu, colds and viruses to others is also harmful. These germs can attack our bodies, but have no legal right to enter or stay in our bodies. We must drive them out by claiming the promises of healing in God's Word, speaking to the sickness and commanding it to leave in Jesus' Name.

Once, I received a healing in my body. I had fungus in several of my toes and was told by my doctor and pharmacist that it was difficult to treat. Soaking your feet in certain solutions is one recommendation, but it is a long process for any real healing. Speaking to the fungus, I said, "I curse you fungus in the Name of Jesus Christ. Dry up and come out of my toes in Jesus' Name "NOW". Thank You Lord." I forgot about my request to the Lord. A few weeks later healing had manifested in my toes. It is so important to put your requests out of your mind, once you release your faith, and thank God and praise Him for your healing.

From colds to cancer, germs are foreign to our bodies and have no right to be there. Often people have been so use to being sick that they think it is part of their lives and do not resist it, and become complacent. Jesus gave us the answer in His Word and it is up to us to use His Word to free ourselves from sickness and disease. In truth, we do not ask God to heal us because we were healed 2,000 years ago, when Jesus took 39 stripes upon His back for our healing.

Who his own self bare our sins in his own body on the tree, that we, being dead to sins, should live unto righteousness by whose stripes ye were healed. (1 Peter 2:24)

Notice that by His stripes you were healed. You are the well person that Satan is trying to make sick, not the sick person trying to get healed. You speak God's Word about healing or any other matter about which you pray. You speak the Word not the problem. Remember when Jesus was led into the wilderness and was tempted by Satan. Jesus always answered Satan by using God's Word. He once said that "Man shall not live by bread alone," but by every word spoken by God.

But he answered and said, It is written, Man shall not live by bread alone, but by every word that proceedeth out of the mouth of God.

(Matthew 4:4)

For every need and problem in your life, use only God's Word, not your thoughts and opinions or those of others. God is only compelled to honor His Word and is not obligated to help you, unless you use His Word.

Look up, read and meditate on the healing scriptures, until they become a part of you by strengthening your faith. Remember, faith comes by your hearing and the hearing according to the Word of God.

So then faith cometh by hearing, and hearing by the word of God. (Romans 10:17)

Read the scriptures out loud to place them into your very spirit. Then when you speak the words against the sickness or disease in your body, your faith in the Word of God and the words you speak will cause change to take place.

(As it is written, I have made thee a father of many nations,) before him whom he believed, even God, who quickeneth the dead, and calleth those things which be not as though they were. (Romans 4:17)

Before you come to the Lord to request anything, make sure that you have no unconfessed sin and a pure heart with no unforgiveness. Then you can release your faith and know that you will have what you desire from God.

For if our heart condemn us, God is greater than our heart and knoweth all things. Beloved, if our heart condemn us not, then have we confidence toward God. (1John 3:20-21)

And this is the confidence that we have in him, that, if we ask any thing according to his will, he heareth us: And if we know that he hear us, whatsoever we ask, we know that we have the petitions that we desired of him.

(1 John 5:14-15)

Your healing begins in the Spirit World, even if it does not immediately show in your physical body. It is at that time you receive whatever you need, and then that need will manifest in your body.

Therefore I say unto you, What things soever ye desire, when ye pray, believe that ye receive them, and ye shall have them. (Mark 11:24)

This Scripture is a fine example of patience which is a twin to faith. If you truly continue to believe in patience, you will receive whatever you desire.

Cast not away therefore your confidence, which hath great recompence of reward. For ye have need of patience, that, after ye have done the will of God, ye might receive the promise.

(Hebrews 10:35-36)

Many people miss their healing when they do not receive the manifestation immediately, they must have faith and stand in patience until it manifests. Words have power. We can lose our healing by speaking negative words like: "I don't think God healed me because I still feel the same" or "I don't see any difference so I guess I wasn't healed after all." Other statements like: "I don't know if I have it," "I feel so bad," "I still feel it Lord. You didn't heal me," or "Why don't I have it?" Negative words will nullify our faith and any expected results, because life and death are proven by our spoken words.

Death and life are in the power of the tongue: and they that love it shall eat the fruit thereof.

(Proverbs 18:21)

Remember Satan came to steal, kill and destroy so be on guard with your emotions, feelings, circumstances, and people upsetting you to get you into hate and unforgiveness. Satan will try to stop your healing any way he can do it, and he will try.

The thief cometh not, but for to steal, and to kill, and to destroy: I am come that they might have life, and that they might have it more abundantly. (John 10:10)

You must decide to not let anything stop you from your goal of healing in your body. When you are truly determined to stand no matter what the circumstances, you will not have to stand long until your healing will manifest.

Satan again will try to steal your healing by symptoms in your body that were there when you were ill. He will try to get you to believe, "Well, I did not really get healed because the sickness returned." You must claim and believe God's promises to you that affliction will not return a second time.

What do ye imagine against the Lord? he will make an utter end: affliction shall not rise up the second time. (Nahum 1:9)

Use God's Word in all that with which you deal in life. Then He will come into your situation and take care of it. Do not let Satan steal your healing from you, by speaking words of doubt and unbelief.

Healing is sometimes miraculous and instant and other times it is a process that is revealed, over a period of time. When faith is released it always immediately begins in the Spirit World and continues to move into the Physical World as long as we keep the faith light turned on. We must continue to stand knowing that we are healed and not give up until the manifestation is complete. We live in a "microwave world" that wants everything immediately, but in God's Kingdom things do not always happen immediately.

A few years ago I had a problem with high blood pressure and took medication for it. I took authority over the affliction and commanded the high blood pressure to become normal in the name of Jesus. I continued to believe for my healing even though I did not see the immediate results. My blood pressure became normal within a few months because of my believing God's Word and is better than normal today.

When Jesus cursed the fig tree, He and the disciples went by the next day and found it dried up. It didn't dry up and wither immediately.

And in the morning, as they passed by, they saw the fig tree dried up from the roots.

(Mark 11:20)

The ten lepers were not healed instantly, but only as they went.

And when he saw them, he said unto them, Go shew yourselves unto the priests. And it came to pass, that, as they went, they were cleansed.

(Luke 17:14)

In conclusion, God wants us healthy in our spirit. Our spirits are the real us: Soul or mind, seat of our emotions, our will, and our body, where we live. Anything not working the way God created it to function, He wants to heal and make whole, and to be healed in the Name of Jesus.

8

Conditional Eternal Security

Gaining Eternal Security is when we receive Jesus Christ as our Lord and Savior. It is conditional as are all the promises of God to His children. We are kept by the power of God through faith.

Who are kept by the power of God through faith unto salvation ready to be revealed in the last time. (1Peter 1:5)

Our faith in Jesus Christ is the keeping power in our relationship to God. For example, using a rope as faith, God is on one end and we as individuals are on the other end. If we turn the rope loose and depart, we are no longer connected to God.

We are connected to God, and we are in Him. He is in us by our faith in Jesus Christ as our Lord and Savior; to depart from it means that we are no longer in God or Him in us.

Some Christians believe that once you are saved, you are always saved, no matter what you do (Unconditional Eternal Security). If you return to the world, these Christians say that you were never saved in the first place; this is false teaching. God's Word says that some will depart from the faith in the last days and give heed to seducing spirits. You must guard yourself against departing from the faith and going back into the world. You must obey God's Word and ask Him to forgive your sins when you recognize them in your life. Do not let your sins accumulate and separate you from the presence of God.

Now the Spirit speaketh expressly, that in the latter times some shall depart from the faith, giving heed to seducing spirits, and doctrines of devils; (1Timothy 4:1)

If we confess our sins, he is faithful and just to forgive us our sins, and to cleanse us from all unrighteousness. (1 John 1:9)

We are told that we must continue in our faith to not be blamed for sinful behavior and obey the leading of the Holy Spirit.

In the body of his flesh through death, to present you holy and unblameable and unreproveable in his sight: If ye continue in the faith grounded and settled, and be not moved away from the hope of the gospel, which ye have heard, and which was preached to every creature which is under heaven; whereof I Paul am made a minister; (Colossians 1:22-23)

We are born-again Christians, grafted in branches as Gentiles, and the Jewish people are the natural branches.

And if some of the branches be broken off, and thou, being a wild olive tree, wert grafted in among them, and with them partakest of the root and fatness of the olive tree; (Romans 11:17)

The branches were broken off because of unbelief. We are grafted because of our faith in Jesus Christ.

Well; because of unbelief they were broken off, and thou standest by faith. Be not highminded, but fear: (Romans 11:20)

The severity is towards the Jewish people because of unbelief, and goodness towards us who are born again in Christ. If we do not continue in His goodness, we shall also be cut off.

For if God spared not the natural branches, take heed lest he also spare not thee. Behold therefore the goodness and severity of God: on them which fell, severity; but toward thee, goodness, if thou continue in his goodness: otherwise thou also shalt be cut off.

(Romans 11:21-22)

Our names are written in the Lamb's Book of Life, when we receive Jesus Christ as our Lord and Savior.

If our names are taken out of the Book of Life, we will be cast in the Lake of Fire. *And whosoever was not found written in the book of life was cast into the lake of fire.*

(Revelation 20:15)

He that overcometh, the same shall be clothed in white raiment; and I will not blot out his name out of the book of life, but I will confess his name before my Father, and before his angels.

Revelation 3:5)

And if any man shall take away from the words of the book of this prophecy, God shall take away his part out of the book of life, and out of the holy city, and from the things which are written in this book. (Revelation 22:19)

You can lose your salvation. If you are saved, your name is in the Book of Life. To have your name taken out means you are lost. You must continue having faith in the Lord Jesus Christ and live your life pleasing to God.

We do not have God over a barrel, when we get saved. We cannot believe that we can live an ungodly sinful life, do what we want, and not lose out in this life and our eternity. If we come to Jesus and we mean our prayers and commitment to Him in our hearts, then truly, old things will disappear and all things will become new.

Therefore if any man be in Christ, he is a new creature: old things are passed away; behold, all things are become new. (2 Corinthians 5:17)

Our desires will change and the evil things we once did will no longer be a part of our lives. God's spirit will bear witness with our spirits that we are His children.

The Spirit itself beareth witness with our spirit, that we are the children of God:

(Romans 8:16)

If we really have a born-again experience, the Holy Spirit will change our desires and attitude as we allow Him to change us, whether it is a large or small change. If no change, then what we spoke were just words, delivered from our minds. If there is a change, then the words said were truly from our hearts. Some people experience drastic changes, others smaller, and it depends on how much we really give of ourselves to Jesus Christ. The more we give of ourselves and our lifestyle to Him, the more He gives of Himself to us. Then we can reflect more of Jesus in our lives. Many times people deep in sin, drugs, crime, sexual and strong addictions tend to show themselves with bigger and more noticeable changes than those who led a more moral life. They know what they were and felt the delivering power of God setting them free, and where they are now.

A great comfort regarding living for Jesus Christ and serving Him is: Now, we will receive no condemnation if we do not embrace selfish, fleshly desires, but obey God's Word and follow the leading of the Holy Spirit in our lives.

There is therefore now no condemnation to them which are in Christ Jesus, who walk not after the flesh, but after the Spirit. (Romans 8:1)

We will never reach perfection in this life, but we should press towards the mark to do the best we can for Jesus.

Brethren, I count not myself to have apprehended; but this one thing I do, forgetting those things which are behind, and reaching forth unto those things which are before, I press toward the mark for the prize of the high calling of God in Christ Jesus. (Philippians 3:13-14)

To walk with Jesus, this way, reaching for new things, we become less sinful and better in our hearing God and following the Holy Spirit. We go from glory to glory. Do not blame yourself, if you sin or make a mistake. Ask God for forgiveness of your sin. Learn from your forgiveness, and from your mistakes, so that you will not make the same ones again.

If we confess our sins, he is faithful and just to forgive us our sins, and to cleanse us from all unrighteousness. (1 John 1:9)

Receive God's forgiveness and forgive yourself. Hold your head up high and begin walking again with a clean record. The key is to never quit, for you will always receive a fresh start from God—receive it, believe it and act on it. When you walk in this manner with Jesus, there are still dangers lurking. You may be hit by the enemy and fall down. Whatever happens to you, you must get back up and face any adversity. Remember, winners "never quit" and quitters "never win."

9

Testimony of Our Family's Dove Experience

About thirty years ago when my wife and I and family lived in Maryland, we had a bus trip lined up to go to Heritage USA, Charlotte, North Carolina, and visit the Jim and Tammy Bakker Ministry.

We planned to leave Wednesday morning at 12:00 a.m. On the Monday just a little over one day before our trip, my wife got sick, the flu. We called the lady that chartered the trip and told her that we would have to cancel our trip. My wife was very sick, throwing up, and couldn't keep anything in her stomach. I prayed with my wife that day and around 11:30 p.m. Monday night just twenty-four hours before we were to have taken our trip, my wife was healed and of all things, she ate a fried egg sandwich.

As a true evidence of her healing, she told me to call the lady, her name was Linda and was a friend of ours and tell her we would go on the trip. I told my wife there were only four seats left which was for our family, and only one big Chalet Room for our lodging at Heritage USA and I thought that at the last minute, our bus seats as well as our room would no longer be available. To my surprise they were still open, so we praised and thanked God for my wife's healing as well as being able to reclaim our original seats and Chalet Room.

The next day I was outside of my home washing my daughters bicycles, my wife and daughters were in the car getting ready to go shopping for our trip at midnight to Heritage USA in Charlotte, North Carolina. My wife and I noticed a bird in a tree, and my wife said that it appeared as if it was talking to me. Well I questioned that, and she said, "Call it over to you," so I did, surprisingly the bird flew and landed on top of my head, and immediately, I thought of Jesus when the Spirit of God like a dove landed upon Jesus.

And Jesus, when he was baptized, went up straightway out of the water: and, lo, the heavens were opened unto him, and he saw the Spirit of God descending like a dove, and lighting upon him: (Matthew 3:16)

I then put my arm out, and the bird perched on it and I took it over to my wife and daughters who were in the car. The bird was calm and stayed there with us, then I walked over and put the bird down to drink some water that was on the ground while I went in to get something to feed it, but then the bird flew away. The bird was with us several minutes, but we didn't know what kind of a bird it was, we didn't know yet.

We left at midnight for our trip and all went well, we checked in at our Chalet and there we met a lady named Becky. She wasn't supposed to have been by our Chalet, she was scheduled for somewhere else, but was there for a divine appointment for all of us that God arranged as well as making sure that we came on the trip well and ready to accomplish His plans for us which we didn't know at the time.

My wife and I told Becky of my bird experience, and described the bird to her. She told us that it just so happened that she had two tame doves given to her and was studying about doves. She told us that it was a Pied Dove, the kind of dove that Noah sent out to scour the land while he and his family and all that were in the Ark would know when it was safe to get out of the Ark.

Another thing she said was that this was a wild dove, and not a tame one, and that you couldn't get a tame dove to land on your arm, and definitely not a wild dove because they are a bulky bird. She told us a bird trainer couldn't get tame doves to land on his arm, and I not being a bird trainer plus it was a wild dove was impossible, but with God all things are possible. I believe that it was a sign that we were headed the right direction coming to the Charlotte area for the work that God had planned for us.

I told some of the leaders at Heritage USA about my experience and they were amazed.

Getting back to Becky, she answered our questions about the bird being a Pied Dove, and how miraculous this experience was. Becky had not received the Baptism of the Holy Spirit, so my wife and I ministered to her, and she received the Baptism of the Holy Spirit with the evidence of speaking in tongues and was slain in the Spirit, and literally pinned to the floor because she told us that she could not get up, for about an hour. All night we heard her laughing and snickering in the room under us, she had quite an experience with the Holy Ghost.

In closing, God had a purpose for all of us, and when He has something for us, He will move Heaven and earth if need be to accomplish His purpose in our lives. Since then I have seen the hand of God move mightily in my life as well as the ministry that He has given me. But I know the best is yet to come for me and not only me, but everyone that will be obedient to God's Word and be willing to do His Plan for their lives.

10

How to Deal With Persecution

A promise of God is given to us. This promise given to us by God will bring every born-again believer persecution.

Yea, and all that will live godly in Christ Jesus shall suffer persecution. (2 Timothy 3:12)

What is persecution? This word means: To relentlessly attack a person, so as to injure or distress especially for reason of religion, politics, or race.

When wanting to have more patience, you should never ask for it, because by living the godly life, you will have many opportunities to experience the need for patience.

We as Christians must realize that our enemy is not people, but Satan's evil tactics against us.

For we wrestle not against flesh and blood, but against principalities, against powers, against the rulers of the darkness of this world, against spiritual wickedness in high places.

(Ephesians 6:12)

We must know who our enemy is before going to war. Just remember, the battle is the Lord's, and not ours.

And all this assembly shall know that the LORD saveth not with sword and spear: for the battle is the LORD'S, and he will give you into our hands. (1 Samuel 17:47)

The only battle we fight is the good fight of faith. Putting into practice the Word of God (Bible) is our real battle with everything and everyone that tries to stop or discourage us from our efforts to win battles over our selfish will, Satan, the world, and sometimes even family and friends.

Fight the good fight of faith, lay hold on eternal life, whereunto thou art also called, and hast professed a good profession before many witnesses. (1 Timothy 6:12)

Many times because of persecution, Christians stop serving God or become bitter. They begin to fear dealing with the things that will come to all of God's servants who are living for Jesus. Unless we can conquer this hurdle in our lives, we will only have an up-and-down Christian life. When we learn how to deal with the opposing forces, then we will be able to go forth and not be affected or stopped. We must realize that Satan will try to stop us in any way, through anyone, anywhere, at any time, or any place. These attacks are part of the price we pay for our obedience and service to Jesus Christ. The greater we are used by the Lord, the more opposition will come against us because we pose a bigger dire threat to Satan.

We must learn that persecution is part of our opposition in our service to God. We as Christians are to consider Jesus Christ, who endured such contradiction of sinners against himself, or chances are that we may become weary in body and faint in mind.

For consider him that endured such contradiction of sinners against himself, lest ye be wearied and faint in your minds.

(Hebrews (12:3)

We learn that example Jesus Christ suffered these contradictions. We must live and do as He did and work for good results He did give to us what He told us we were to have, and we are to do what He told us to do. As well, we will reap some of His sufferings. Many times we want the good things that God has promised us through Jesus, but we are unwilling to suffer the hardship that goes along with this reward. Remember, the servant is not greater than his Lord. If the enemies persecuted Jesus, they will also persecute us.

Remember the word that I said unto you, The servant is not greater than his lord. If they have persecuted me, they will also persecute you; if they have kept my saying, they will keep yours also. (John 15:20)

The attitude that you have, when facing your persecution, will determine your victory or defeat. Your mindset and attitude should be that you are blessed, when men revile, persecute you and falsely say all manner of evil against you, for the Gospel's sake.

Blessed are ye, when men shall revile you, and persecute you, and shall say all manner of evil against you falsely, for my sake. (Matthew 5:11)

Consider Jesus and know that as long as you please the Lord, it does not matter what people think or say about you. If God is for you, who can be against you?

What shall we then say to these things? If God be for us, who can be against us? (Romans 8:31)

Persecution comes many times when people living an ungodly life, who are convicted, not only by their words, but the anointing of God in them which they sense by their very presence. For Example: Did you ever come in contact with someone you did not know or know well—someone who started opening their heart to you, they might say, "I don't know why I'm saying this to you." Well, that is the presence of the Holy Spirit in and on your life that causes this to happen which is good. Many times people will sense something different about you. If they say a bad word or something wrong, they will apologize to you, even if they do not know you. Is that not the way we should all be seen by the world, as different and peculiar godly people?

Have you ever met someone you do not know who seems to be angry with you. Their anger may cause them to snap at you for no reason. Sometimes that is the Satan in them, and Satan hates the Jesus in you. Then Satan reacts to you from that person's hate. The Anointing of God on and in your life will bring people to you or will turn them away. As you read the Gospels, you will learn that this is exactly what happened to Jesus.

We need to ask God to give us wisdom for to whom we can talk to and share things. Sometimes even those closest to us become jealous and react in ways toward us that are not pleasing to God.

And Jesus answered and said, Verily I say unto you, There is no man that hath left house, or brethren, or sisters, or father, or mother, or wife, or children, or lands, for my sake, and the gospel's, But he shall receive an hundredfold now in this time, houses, and brethren, and sisters, and mothers, and children, and lands, with persecutions; and in the world to come eternal life. (Mark 10:29-30)

This Scripture quote shows us along with the hundredfold promise, that it will be accompanied with persecutions such as jealously and accusations of ill-gotten gain, claiming that you love money more than God, cheated to get what you wanted. People many times say hurtful things about others who prosper spiritually, financially in business, or anyone who succeeds in life. The hurtful persecutions they speak with envy, jealously, or because they have not succeeded or even tried to do so. They resent someone who is successful. Remember, it was the Father's Will that Jesus went to the Cross for us, but it was through lies and misrepresentation by people that brought Jesus to the Cross. We are to rejoice and thank God for other Christians who achieve things in life because of their commitment to God and their faith in His Word.

To simplify what is really happening to you: If you are an obedient Christian and following

Jesus, it is the Satan in people and circumstances coming against God in you. Do not take Satan's hate against you personally, as it is not you, but who and what you represent. When confronted with persecution, people many times start to blame themselves and develop an inferiority complex or think that there is something wrong with them. If you are truly living and doing as God told you in His Word, you will be different, a peculiar person.

Who gave himself for us, that he might redeem us from all iniquity, and purify unto himself a peculiar people, zealous of good works.

(Titus 2:14)

Take pleasure in the fact that you are pleasing God, and that is all that matters. You must recognize that it is not people or things coming against you, but Satan. Bind him in the name of Jesus Christ and cast him out of the situation, as you pray for people and the situation with which you are dealing. Satan is your enemy, not people. The battle is between God and Satan. You represent Jesus Christ, so Satan hates you and wants to destroy you since he cannot hurt God.

Persecution exists because we did wrong, and persecution also exists because we are doing right. If we are persecuted for doing wrong, we need to ask forgiveness from God and from the people involved, and then do what is right. If we are persecuted for doing right, then rejoice and thank God that we are showing Jesus in our lives and worthy to be persecuted. In persecution we are exposed for doing wrong, so we can correct it. But sometimes God will cause us to be persecuted, when we are doing wrong, if He cannot get our attention any other way to correct a wrong in our lives. When we are doing right, this is a confirmation to us that Satan is angry because we are effective against him. Rejoice in that we are worthy to be persecuted for the gospel's sake.

Persecution either corrects us when we are wrong, or confirms to us when we are doing things God's way. It is painful to be persecuted, but if we can keep in mind what it really is about, it can be very beneficial to us.

11

Dealing with Fear

Fear is the anxiety and agitation caused by the presence of danger, evil, pain and uncertainties. There are 2 types of fear, normal fear and abnormal fear. Normal fear is being afraid to walk in front of a speeding truck, jump off a tall building, or put your hands in a fire. This is a normal fear and a good one, for without it we would destroy ourselves. Abnormal fear is fear of the dark, fear of driving your car, fear of losing your job, fear of getting sick, and many others. These fears are normal to most people today, and they live with them daily, including many Christians.

Fear stops and hinders you from going forward. It torments your mind and will consume you if you do not deal with what you fear. It becomes the center of your attention and will become your god. When you fear, God will become smaller to you, because to what you give your attention, and meditate on, will be to what you adjust your life and how you live. To meditate on God's Word day and night, you will make your life prosperous and successful.

This book of the law shall not depart out of thy mouth; but thou shalt meditate therein day and night, that thou mayest observe to do according to all that is written therein: for then thou shalt make thy way prosperous, and then thou shalt have good success. (Joshua 1:8)

The Bible tells us that God did not give born-again believers the spirit of fear.

For God hath not given us the spirit of fear; but of power, and of love, and of a sound mind.

(2 Timothy 1:7)

Fear is listening to the words of Satan and looking on the negative side of life, afraid of losing something or fear of something going wrong in your life or the lives of those around you. Fear begins with thoughts in your mind that must be dealt with. You are to cast down all thoughts and imaginations that are contrary to God's Word, as soon as a negative thought comes your way.

Casting down imaginations, and every high thing that exalteth itself against the knowledge of God, and bringing into captivity every thought to the obedience of Christ; (2 Corinthians 10:5)

When you have wrong thoughts that come to you, what matters is when and how you deal with them. It is like the old saying, "You cannot keep birds from flying over your head, but you can stop them from landing on your head." You should react to wrong thoughts like you do with mosquitoes. If a mosquito lands on your arm, immediately, you slap it to get it away from you. You need to act the same way with negative thoughts and imaginations, when they come your way and that act should be your real spiritual reaction.

Our growth and maturity in the Word and Love of God will diminish fear in our lives. Where light is, darkness cannot be, so the more we walk in the light, the less hold all fears will have on us.

There is no fear in love; but perfect love casteth out fear: because fear hath torment. He that feareth is not made perfect in love.

(1 John 4:18)

When we are made perfect in love, we will not experience fear, because light and darkness cannot abide together, as darkness will flee. When we go into a dark room and turn on the switch, immediately darkness goes and the light shines; this is also the way it is spiritually. When we know the Love of God towards us as well as His Promises to us, the more we mature, the less we fear. It is God's Will that we do not fear. Jesus said many times in the four gospels, "FEAR NOT," the reason being He knew that this would be a problem area for His followers. Jesus told us to Fear Not those who can only kill the body, but fear God who can both destroy soul and body in Hell.

And fear not them which kill the body, but are not able to kill the soul: but rather fear him which is able to destroy both soul and body in hell.

(Matthew 10:28)

Faith comes by hearing and listening to God's Word and fear comes by listening to the words of Satan. Listen only to God's Word and pay no attention to anything that is contrary to it and CAST IT DOWN. Our eyes and ears are for God's Word only, never for Satan's word. So faith is the product of hearing and giving heed to the Word of God and fear is the product of hearing and giving heed to Satan's word. We must choose and take action to combat Satan's attack on us in his attempts to make us fear.

So then faith cometh by hearing, and hearing by the word of God. (Romans 10:17)

I have found that reading the Bible out loud is the best way to read all of God's Word, because of the creative power of God's Word. Remember, He spoke the world into existence, and also out loud for our hearing it. As we say it out loud, "GOD DID NOT GIVE ME A SPIRIT OF FEAR, BUT OF POWER, LOVE AND OF A SOUND MIND," even shout it, we can feel faith and boldness rising up inside our spirit man. DO IT NOW BEFORE YOU READ ANY FURTHER!

Remember the twelve spies that Moses sent out to search the land of Canaan? It was because of fear that ten returned and said: "We cannot go up against the people, for they are stronger than we are."

But the men that went up with him said, We be not able to go up against the people; for they are stronger than we.... And there we saw the giants, the sons of Anak, which come of the giants: and we were in our own sight as grasshoppers, and so we were in their sight.

(Numbers 13:31, 33)

The ten spies were listening to Satan's words and reacted negatively with a fear report. Joshua and Caleb were listening to God's Word and gave a faith report. The end result was because they went forth in faith, Joshua and Caleb entered into the Promised Land. But the ten other spies died of the plague.

And Caleb stilled the people before Moses, and said, Let us go up at once, and possess it; for we are well able to overcome it. (Numbers 13:30)

Even those men that did bring up the evil report upon the land, died by the plague before the Lord. (Numbers 14:37)

If the evil report of the ten spies had been obeyed, then Israel would not ever have gotten to the Promised Land. Fear could have stopped Israel from entering the land of Canaan, but faith got the job done.

When we allow fear to govern our lives, we are not the only ones affected, as we affect those around us. The same goes for faith. As we allow faith to govern our lives, we will affect others in a positive, helpful, and encouraging manner. Fear will destroy us, but faith will place us into Kingdom Living.

I want to make fear in your life simple to understand. There is no hope outside of Jesus Christ if He is not your Lord and Savior. If fear is in your life, you either do not have the knowledge for the answer to your problems or simply do not believe God's Word and in unbelief regarding the issue about which you have fear; it is that simple. Faith brings lasting peace and positive results. Fear brings great torment and a worse situation, as you continue to hold it. Step out and believe God's Word. Use your faith and disregard circumstances, people's ideas, your emotions and feelings, and expect God to move on your behalf. Faith is for the born-again believer and fear is for the unbeliever until they accept Jesus Christ as Lord and Savior

My people are destroyed for lack of knowledge: because thou has rejected knowledge, I will also reject thee, that thou shalt be no priest to me: seeing thou hast forgotten the law of thy God, I will also forget thy children.

(Hosea 4:6)

In order to face fear you must make a quality decision about faith, so that you will live your life in accordance with the Word of God. Your statement of faith must be: I will not be moved by what I see, feel, hear, or my circumstances. I will be moved only by what the Word of God says!

12

Honoring Our Word and the Word of God

There is an old saying, "Sticks and stones may break my bones, but words will never hurt me." The person or persons who voiced that maxim did not know anything about the Word of God. God created the world and creation by His Words beginning with, "Let there be light" or "Light be."

And God said, Let there be light: and there was light. (Genesis 1:3)

There is a creative power in words, so it is extremely important to learn how we use them, for they will produce life or death. As well, by words we are justified or condemned.

For by thy words thou shalt be justified, and by thy words thou shalt be condemned.

(Matthew 12:37)

I will deal with two types of words in this chapter. First, will be our word, then God's Word. Our word and words will govern the affectivity of God's Word in our life. It is so important to God that He has magnified His

Word above His Name. Thus, we will see that our word is our name and what and who we are.

I will worship toward thy holy temple, and praise thy name for thy lovingkindness and for thy truth: for thou hast magnified thy word above all thy name. (Psalms 138:2)

Our integrity is in our word or words to others and how we honor these persons. When we make a promise or commitment to someone, we are to keep it, no matter how much it hurts us.

In whose eyes a vile person is contemned; but he honoureth them that fear the LORD. He that sweareth to his own hurt, and changeth not.

(Psalms 15:4)

We are to be as good as our word, no matter what the cost. For example: We agree to sell someone an automobile for $3000. They tell us that they will have the money in a week, so we agree to sell them the car one week later. Meanwhile, three days later someone comes to us and offers $4500 on the spot. The right thing to do would be to tell the person that we already have a commitment, but if the other person backs out then we will get back to them. By making this promise, we will be honoring our word to the first person by leaving the transaction of the sale open, in case they back out of the deal; this is the right thing to do. If, however we cancel our agreement and take the $4500, that would show lack of integrity on our part even though we could do it without anybody knowing what was happening—but God knows. By doing the right thing, we would lose $1500 profit which is swearing to our own hurt, but we would please God. We will come out ahead and possibly get away with being dishonest with man, but God is watching us deceive him and judges our character. Our honest integrity and true character come out, when no one is looking. Just remember that God watches everything we do.

We need to weigh our words, before we speak, because once the words are spoken, they are out there forever. Many times people just say the things others want to hear for the purpose of blending in with the crowd or to be accepted by others.

Make certain we speak positive words and be truthful to others. When we tell someone we are going to do something, then do the things we promised or let them know that we are not capable of fulfilling our word. For example: If we have not seen someone in a while, then say to them, "We're going to have to get together soon," knowing in our heart that we do not want to visit with them. But we make that promise to save face or to appease them by lying and being dishonest. We should not make promises that we do not intend to keep. We should keep the promises we make to others by doing what we promise to do.

I am sure everyone often says that their mouth sometimes gets them into trouble. The perfect man is one who never offends in word.

For in many things we offend all. If any man offend not in word, the same is a perfect man, and able also to bridle the whole body.

(James 3:2)

92

The tongue is unruly, evil, and full of deadly poison, and no man can tame it.

But the tongue can no man tame; it is an unruly evil, full of deadly poison. (James 3:8)

We bless God and curse man.

Therewith bless we God, even the Father; and therewith curse we men, which are made after the similitude of God. (James 3:9)

We bless and curse with words out of the same mouth and this should not be. The only way we can combat this evil practice is to renew our minds with God's Word and determine that we are going to walk in love towards everyone and be obedient to the leading of the Lord. Ask God to take over our mouths and show us when to speak and when not to. Always speak in love, when talking to people even if they have hurt us in some way or are ungodly or evil. Our goal is to lead them to Jesus and see them set free and delivered from sin and bondage and not condemn them. If they knew and obeyed Jesus, they would not be doing ungodly things. We can stop wrath from occurring by our words. Build up with positive words to others; do not tear down with negative words.

A SOFT answer turneth away wrath: but grievous words stir up anger. (Proverbs 15:1)

In times past a person's word was their bond. In today's world we have contracts and all types of legal paperwork for marriages, businesses, divorces, alimony, child support, and much more, all because people do not honor their commitments to one another and try to cheat in their dealings. We as Christians need to set the example with integrity and honor toward one another by our words and commitments to each other. Be as good as our word; God is, and He expects us to also be!

The next thing is God's Word which is forever settled in Heaven.

For ever, O LORD, thy word is settled in heaven. (Psalms 119:89)

Jesus Christ never changes; He is the same yesterday, today, and forever.

Jesus Christ the same yesterday, and to day, and for ever. (Hebrews 13:8)

God's Word does not change with the times or with different societies. The Bible still means what it says and says what it means, with no changes; it is unchangeable. Jesus said that we are not to live by bread alone, but by every word that proceeds out of the mouth of God.

But he answered and said, It is written, Man shall not live by bread alone, but by every word that proceedeth out of the mouth of God.

(Matthew 4:4)

All scripture is given by the inspiration of God.

All scripture is given by inspiration of God, and is profitable for doctrine, for reproof, for correction, for instruction in righteousness: That the man of God may be perfect, thoroughly furnished unto all good works.

(2 Timothy 3:16-17)

We are to study to show ourselves approved and meditate on the Word of God day and night.

Study to shew thyself approved unto God, a workman that needeth not to be ashamed, rightly dividing the word of truth. (2 Timothy 2:15)

This book of the law shall not depart out of thy mouth; but thou shalt meditate therein day and night, that thou mayest observe to do according to all that is written therein: for then thou shalt make thy way prosperous, and then thou shalt have good success. (Joshua 1:8)

Every answer to life is in God's Word. We must seek and find the answers of which we have need. As we read and apply God's Word in our lives and let it govern our lifestyle, then our lives will change and reflect Jesus Christ to others.

Saying God's Word is extremely important. God called the things that are not as though they were.

(As it is written, I have made thee a father of many nations,) before him whom he believed, even God, who quickeneth the dead, and calleth those things which be not as though they were.

(Romans 4:17)

Our faith is what we use to receive from God, but we need to speak it as God did for creation. As well, we must learn to speak to our mountains in life.

For verily I say unto you, That whosoever shall say unto this mountain, Be thou removed, and be thou cast into the sea; and shall not doubt in his heart, but shall believe that those things which he saith shall come to pass; he shall have whatsoever he saith. (Mark 11:23)

Notice that the word "believe" is there one time, and the word "say" is there once. And "saith" is there twice, referring to our speaking to our mountains in life to receive from God; that is a 3 to 1 ratio, "say" 3 times and "believe"

95

1 time. This ratio shows us the importance of saying what we believe, because there is a creative force in speaking that will cause the words to manifest, when we are using our faith, as they are faith-filled words.

I can do all things through Christ which strengtheneth me. (Philippians 4:13)

Speak words out loud and boldly a few times and notice how your spirit man will rise up, when you speak God's Words from the Bible. You will become bolder, and the powerful words will become real to you. It is easy to simply read and believe in your heart, but many times you forget that you need to speak the Word of God out loud and know that it will not return void, but will accomplish what it says it will do.

So shall my word be that goeth forth out of my mouth: it shall not return unto me void, but it shall accomplish that which I please, and it shall prosper in the thing whereto I sent it.

(Isaiah 55:11)

God's Word is His will to me, and when I read the New Testament, I remember that it is the Last Will and Testament and Covenant of Jesus Christ to me personally. Read it and apply the words to yourself as if you were the only person to which it applies. It is your personal heritage from God that He gave you at the death of His Son Jesus Christ and was confirmed by the Resurrection of Jesus that we celebrate on the day called "Easter." I always call Easter, "Resurrection Day." If there would have been no Resurrection, our faith and belief would have been in vain and the Word of God would have no affect on us and thus be powerless. Thank God for the Resurrection that confirms and puts God's Seal on all that His Word tells us—a Word that is all-powerful and all-truth.

But if there be no resurrection of the dead, then is Christ not risen: And if Christ be not risen, then is our preaching vain, and your faith is also vain. (1 Corinthians 15:13-14)

In closing we are to hear, meditate, say, and do the Word of God in our lives. Be doers not only hearers or we will deceive ourselves.

But be ye doers of the word, and not hearers only, deceiving your own selves (James 1:22)

Many times we think that because we know the Word and can quote it, we are pleasing God. The Word is part of our Statement of Faith or Belief System that it is part of us. But remember, the demons also believe with fear and trembling.

Thou believest that there is one God; thou doest well: the devils also believe, and tremble.

(James 2:19)

Unless we obey the Word and apply it to our lives, it is of no value to us. We show our faith by our works, because faith is dead without works.

Yea, a man may say, Thou hast faith, and I have works: shew me thy faith without thy works, and I will shew thee my faith by my works.... But wilt thou know, O vain man, that faith without works is dead? (James 2:18, 20)

The bottom line is: If we believe God's Word, we will exercise faith, do what His Word says and see the results promised by that Word. When farmers plant seed, do they not expect the seeds to turn into the vegetables and that they are supposed to become corn or beans? Each seed is designed to become a certain vegetable, and if planted in good soil and watered, with the right weather, that seed will bring forth a great harvest of that crop. God's Word is the seed. We are the soil, to water, and we speak the Word regarding whatever we believe. Our words must have no negative words of doubt or unbelief and act like we have received and prepare for the manifestation.

When it is our true belief that we receive what our prayers ask, I have noticed in my own life that I do not usually know when my answer to prayer is really manifested. God quickens my mind and shows me the results. A recent example, given in another chapter in this book, was that I had a fungus in my toenails and some began to turn black. The doctor and pharmacist told me that it was hard to get rid of, but said I could try various feet-soaking formulas. The fungus was not painful, so I did not bother doing anything. I cursed the fungus in the Name of Jesus Christ and His Blood, called my toenails healed and did not think about it anymore. I believed God's Promise for healing and received it in my mind. While taking a shower a few weeks later, I saw that they were clear and healthy looking. Then it dawned on me what had happened—God healed them! Thank you, Jesus, Glory to God. Your expectation is God's invitation.

13

Uncover Satanic Influences

Some people say that what you do not know will not hurt you; this is a wrong statement, for my people are destroyed for lack of knowledge.

My people are destroyed for lack of knowledge: because thou has rejected knowledge, I will also reject thee, that thou shalt be no priest to me: seeing thou hast forgotten the law of thy God, I will also forget thy children.

(Hosea 4:6)

Some of Satan's tools are what many people, even Born-Again Christians, are using, not realizing that they are opening a door for Satan to enter.

There shall not be found among you any one that maketh his son or his daughter to pass through the fire, or that useth divination, or an observer of times, or an enchanter, or a witch, Or a charmer, or a consulter with familiar spirits, or a wizard, or a necromancer. For all that do these things are an abomination unto the LORD: and because of these abominations the LORD thy God doth drive them out from before thee.

(Deuteronomy 18:10-12)

One of the most familiar and least-suspected tool is people's beliefs in horoscopes. Seeking out horoscopes in their daily newspapers is a daily practice for many people. First of all we are not to be led or influenced by our birth date, the stars, planets, or any heavenly body, but only by the Spirit of God.

For as many as are led by the Spirit of God, they are the sons of God. (Romans 8:14)

This rigid belief in the truth of horoscopes appears innocent and harmless. Many ask: How can a simple horoscope hurt me? First of all this belief takes God's leadership over your life away Him, and anything that takes you away from God is always wrong. You might say, "Oh, It's just for fun." But if you practice something long enough it will become part of you—good or evil—and will be your source for your answers to life's problems and needs.

Let us find a simple understanding to these false beliefs. Satan duplicates everything God does to confuse us and to get people involved with his plan to destroy us, especially Christians who serve Jesus Christ whom Satan hates and uses us as revenge to dispute Jesus' Words. The following is an example of Satan's duplication: Christmas celebrates the birth of Jesus with Santa Claus; Easter celebrates the Resurrection of Jesus with the Easter Bunny. God's Prophet with the Fortune Teller. What God has given us for His purpose, Satan tries to reproach, stop, confuse, or draw people away from God's purpose for them.

What really attracts people to Satan is when they just do not understand God's Word and truth regarding the situation before them. We were all created with a void in our spirits that only God can fill, and we are intrigued and captivated by the supernatural, because we all have a hunger for it in the very core of our beings. The supernatural in fortunetellers, mediums, horoscopes, Quiji boards, psychics, tarot cards, and ghost stories attracts and lures us, because understanding these is above our ability in the physical realm; it is supernatural. While some of it is phony, but some of it is also real and satanically influenced, because Satan works in the spiritual realm, which we should have nothing to do with, because it is ungodly.

We also must be careful of children's TV programs as well as movies that portray witches and witchcraft put into a cartoon-type of program. Many things look innocent, but when you put people under supernatural power influences, if they are not from God, then they are satanic. Violence today is portrayed not only on TV, but also in computer games and software for children's electronic devices on which they play games. Evil such as monsters, murder, witchcraft, and violence are from Satan. Many toys also are satanically influenced, which is the norm for what is being fed to children today. The sad truth is that most parents either do not see it or choose to do nothing about it. Is it any wonder why kids are acting violent carrying guns to school, bullying other children, being disrespectful to their parents and elders? These toys and games have a negative influence on our children and grandchildren. We all need to examine what we give to them as gifts, because many of these presents are evil, and have a harmful influence on the children that will bring only negative results.

All the above-mentioned practices are purposed to show supernatural power which Satan tries to bring to himself for his glory rather than that of God, from whom All True Power originates. Satan is an imitator and through deception in using these practices, draws many to him not realizing that he is the one behind all these evil practices.

Remember Satan himself is transformed into an angel of light, so do not be deceived by the appearance of him or of the supernatural. Just because it is supernatural and beyond the power of men, does not mean that it is of God. Remember the old expression: "All that glitters is not gold."

And he doeth great wonders, so that he maketh fire come down from heaven on the earth in the sight of men. And deceiveth them that dwell on the earth by the means of those miracles which he had power to do in the sight of the beast; saying to them that dwell on the earth, that they should make an image to the beast, which had the wound by a sword, and did live.

(Revelation 13:13-14)

The above scripture tells us that many signs will appear and miracles will be done during the Seven Year Tribulation Period on this earth, over which the Anti-Christ and false prophet will rule. Always compare everything that is done according to God's Word, and if it is not according to the Word, reject it. The Body of Christ will be raptured or caught up before the

Seven Year Tribulation begins, but much deception is presently being practiced and will grow to be even worse, as time goes on.

After this I looked, and, behold, a door was opened in heaven: and the first voice which I heard was as it were of a trumpet talking with me; which said, Come up hither, and I will shew thee things which must be hereafter.

(Revelation 4:1)

The following scripture tells us that seducing and deceptive spirits that show or proclaim powerful things will lure many away from Jesus, because people do not realize who is behind what they see. God says that His people are destroyed because of lack of knowledge.

My people are destroyed for lack of knowledge: because thou has rejected knowledge, I will also reject thee, that thou shalt be no priest to me: seeing thou hast forgotten the law of thy God, I will also forget thy children.

(Hosea 4:6)

Always go by the leading of the Holy Spirit and the Word of God for everything we see or hear while on this earth. In the days that we now are living, we really need discernment of what is good and what is evil. We should not be led by our emotions, but only by the Holy Spirit and the Word of God.

Many people are looking for answers to their needs and problems that they are experiencing today. Instead of following God's Word, however, they visit fortunetellers, listen to the false words of psychics, and read useless horoscopes. I have seen on TV how the police use psychics to find certain leads, people, and answers in cases they cannot solve. People are actually looking to Satan for answers when they use any of the aforementioned devices named in this chapter. The Gifts of the Spirit are God's vehicles for answers and the supernatural powers and abilities that He uses through His people to meet the needs of mankind. The devices are Satan's counterfeits of God's Gifts of the Spirit. Remember, everything that God has given us for good, Satan counterfeits to lead us away from God and bring reproach upon God's Gifts to His Church.

But the manifestation of the Spirit is given to every man to profit withal. For to one is given by the Spirit the word of wisdom; to another the word of knowledge by the same Spirit; To another faith by the same Spirit; to another the gifts of healing by the same Spirit; To another the working of miracles; to another prophecy; to another discerning of spirits; to another divers kinds of tongues; to another the interpretation of tongues: But all these worketh that one and the selfsame Spirit, dividing to every man severally as he will. (1 Corinthians 12:7-11)

In closing, we should give no place to the devil, but by practicing these evil, satanic devices, we open a door for him to enter our worlds and cause us problems in various areas of our lives. How fortunetellers and psychics at times miss their predictions, shows us without a doubt that it is never God when what is said does not happen nor is not the answer. God is never wrong. So in the case of satanic practices, we know that it is not of God, but of Satan because first of all God's Word declares it, as well as the wrong predictions that at times they all predict. Jesus Christ is the answer to everything that we face. So we must remember: Jesus is the way, the truth, and the life. Look to the Word of God for all your needs and receive from the Father in the Name of Jesus Christ.

God is our refuge and strength, a very present help in trouble. (Psalm 46:1)

14

Peace in the Midst of Trouble

One thing about which everyone will agree is that we live in a troubled world. But the real question is how we live our lives, when we are in the middle of this situation. True peace comes from within and is not governed by our surroundings, our circumstances, or anything happening on the outside of our lives. Jesus Christ gives us peace, not as the world gives, but His peace.

Peace I leave with you, my peace I give unto you: not as the world giveth, give I unto you. Let not your heart be troubled, neither let it be afraid.
(John 14:27)

We are told to let the peace of God rule in our hearts.

And let the peace of God rule in your hearts, to the which also ye are called in one body; and be ye thankful. (Colossians 3:15)

It is a quality decision on our part that does not just happen that we live a life of peace in our hearts, but begins with on which we keep our minds and thoughts. God's Word tells us that

He will keep those in perfect peace whose minds are focused and leaning on Jesus Christ.

Thou wilt keep him in perfect peace, whose mind is stayed on thee: because he trusteth in thee. (Isaiah 26:3)

Our minds must depend on God's Word through Jesus Christ and not on our own ability or strength. We must put our trust in the Lord, and not in man.

It is better to trust in the LORD than to put confidence in man. (Psalms 118:8)

Many people rely on for peace financial independence, a good job, a big bank account, being out of debt, being healthy, finding success in their profession or business, a time when all is going right for them. The bottom line is that people want their circumstances in life to be a certain way, believing that all of these efforts will bring peace. If I had more money, this job, be in this position or that position, I would be happy and find peace. This is a disillusionment that people find whenever they reach these plateaus of wealth, fame, or power, they still are unhappy with no real peace in their lives.

God has given us a huge void in our spirit man that only He can fill. People may use sex, drugs, or alcohol to achieve a level of peace. When they do not reach that level, they think they are without hope and many commit suicide. Only Jesus Christ, the Prince of Peace, can give us true and lasting peace. God has made finding peace in life so simple for mankind, but sadly they look to everyone, everywhere, and try everything else yet do not consider Him. Usually when they reach bottom they cry out to God and at this time of hopelessness is when they come to Jesus Christ to be saved and set free.

The Old Hymn, "What a Friend We Have in Jesus," tells us of the needless things we bear and suffer, because we do not take it to the Lord in prayer. When we receive Jesus as Lord and Savior, nothing or no one can defeat us, if we stand on His Word regarding His promises to us. True and permanent peace comes from simply believing and trusting in God's Word for whatever is our need on the promise that He made to us for our situation.

When you stop trying to do things on your own and allow the Holy Spirit to direct you, block it out of your mind and depend on God to take care of your situation; then you will have peace. Getting yourself out of the picture and putting God in it, brings you peace. You then enter into His rest, because you ceased from doing your own works and allowed Him to take over your situation.

There remaineth therefore a rest to the people of God. For he that is entered into his rest, he also hath ceased from his own works, as God did from his. (Hebrews 4:9-10)

Seeking peace without God will never work, because it depends on your circumstances in life, such as: your finances, job, relationships, and health, all of which can change quickly. The peace Jesus gives you can maintain in spite of all of your circumstances and use your faith to change the negative circumstances in your life according to the promises of God. Peace starts within, then peace without can be dealt with, instead of thinking if you change your circumstances, you will find peace.

Think of the Old Hymn, "Cast Your Eyes upon Jesus." This hymn says that when our eyes are on Him, the things of the world grow dim. When we are in the Secret Place of the Lord all the glitz and glitter and everything in this world are secondary, and all we want is Jesus Christ.

I WILL praise thee, O LORD, with my whole heart; I will shew forth all thy marvelous works.

(Psalms 9:1)

God wants to bless you physically, materially and in every way, as your soul prospers in His word. But the bottom line is: Nothing will have first place with you in your life except Jesus, and He will be the treasure of your heart.

Beloved, I wish above all things that thou mayest prosper and be in health, even as thy soul prospereth. (3 John 2)

God leads you beside the still, peaceful, and restful waters. His pathway will always give you inner peace. No matter what is going on outside in your life, your circumstances or your situations, they will not affect your peace. This is Jesus Peace to you, not as the world gives, but which only He can give.

He maketh me to lie down in green pastures: he leadeth me beside the still waters.

(Psalms 23:2)

When we please God by our obedience to Him, faith in His Word, and allow Him to have complete control of our lives, this pleases Him. We will then have the peace that Jesus promised us in our lives. We are the one who determines reaching that goal.

Peace I leave with you, my peace I give unto you: not as the world giveth, give I unto you. Let not your heart be troubled, neither let it be afraid.

(John 14:27)

15

What Are Christians to Suffer?

A lot of confusion exists in the Body of Christ on the subject of suffering for the Gospel's sake. People think many things such as: When sick or financially poor, they are suffering these for the Gospel's sake. Jesus redeemed us from the curse of the law. Sickness, disease, lack and poverty, and every work of evil that could come against us, by the shedding of His Blood, bearing all these things in His own body, so you and I would not have to bear them.

Christ hath redeemed us from the curse of the law, being made a curse for us: for it is written, Cursed is every one that hangeth on a tree:

(Galatians 3:13)

We have to know who and what our enemy is before we can defeat him. God tells us that His people perish for lack of knowledge.

My people are destroyed for lack of knowledge: because thou has rejected knowledge, I will also reject thee, that thou shalt be no priest to me; seeing thou hast forgotten the law of thy God, I will also forget thy children.

(Hosea 4:6)

If you do not believe that sickness, disease, lack, poverty, and all evil are your enemies and that Jesus made the way for you to overcome these enemies of your life, and think that this is part of your suffering for the Gospel's sake, then Satan will destroy you.

Recognize now that does not mean that these things will not come to hurt and hinder us, but that they do not have the right to exist in our lives. Sickness, disease, poverty, lack, or any evil thing is not of God and must leave us in the name of Jesus Christ. We need to look in God's Word to see the promises that He gave us, so that when these misfortunes come against us, we do what God's Word tells us, and rid ourselves of these hurtful and harmful destructive things that try to destroy us. Remember, that Jesus on the Cross, shed His Blood, Died, was Buried, and Resurrected so that we would be free. In truth 2,000 years ago this was all paid for, so in reality past tense "we were healed," no lack because "The Lord is my Shepherd, I shall not want." All we have to do is receive by faith for what Jesus already paid at Calvary and walk in it.

Who his own self bare our sins in his own body on the tree, that we, being dead to sins, should live unto righteousness: by whose stripes ye were healed. (1 Peter 2:24)

The LORD is my shepherd; I shall not want.

(Psalms 23:1)

Beloved, I wish above all things that thou mayest prosper and be in health, even as thy soul prospereth. (3 John 2)

God gives us power to get wealth so that we can establish His Covenant.

But thou shalt remember the LORD thy God: for it is he that giveth thee power to get wealth, that he may establish his covenant which he sware unto thy fathers, as it is this day.

(Deuteronomy 8:18)

God's desire is that we grow and prosper in His Word to us, that we may serve Him and do the things that Jesus did. We are called to finish Jesus' mission while He was on this earth. Jesus was thrust into a lost, hurt, evil, and dying world. Bringing them to Him, also prospered us financially, and a chance for us to be healthy in our bodies which are the temple of the Holy Ghost.

Verily, verily, I say unto you, He that believeth on me, the works that I do shall he do also; and greater works than these shall he do; because I go unto my Father. (John 14:12)

What? Know ye not that your body is the temple of the Holy Ghost which is in you, which ye have of God, and ye are not your own? For ye are bought with a price: therefore glorify God in your body, and in your spirit, which are God's.

(1 Corinthians 6:19, 20)

All things contrary to God's Word, recognize them as your enemy. Find the promise of God that relates to your need, claim it in the name of Jesus Christ, believe that you receive it, confess it, say no negative words that would negate your faith, thank God for the promise and consider it done and act like you have it, being determined that it will manifest in your life. You must keep

113

faith and be steadfast in patience until it manifests.

Therefore I say unto you, What things soever ye desire, when ye pray, believe that ye receive them, and ye shall have them. (Mark 11:24)

Cast not away therefore your confidence, which hath great recompence of reward. For ye have need of patience, that, after ye have done the will of God, ye might receive the promise.
(Hebrews 10:35-36)

Now that we have determined that sickness, disease, lack, poverty, and all evil are things that we are not to tolerate in our lives, but should be set free from them. Know the truth, and the truth shall make you free. Live a victorious life, reflecting Jesus to the world by your lifestyle and by your words. Bring them to Jesus.

And ye shall know the truth, and the truth shall make you free. (John 8:32)

The battle is not ours but that of the Lords. What we are to do is to fight the good fight of faith, which brings suffering.

And all this assembly shall know that the LORD saveth not with sword and spear: for the battle is the LORD'S, and he will give you into our hands. (1 Samuel 17:47)

Fight the good fight of faith, lay hold on eternal life, whereunto thou art also called, and hast professed a good profession before many witnesses. (1Timothy 6:12)

As we give ourselves to the Lord and obey His Word, we are denying our flesh. The world comes against us, and persecutes us, Satan attacks us, and within the church many times some will come against us. Just in obedience to

114

the Word of God we automatically become a target for Satan, because he wants to stop us with whoever and whatever he can use to do it.

The Bible tells us that those who live godly in Christ Jesus shall suffer persecution.

Yea, and all that will live godly in Christ Jesus shall suffer persecution. (2 Timothy 3:12)

The more effective you become for Jesus Christ, the more of a threat you are to Satan, and he will come after you in a stronger way. Remember the old expression, "If you cannot stand the heat, get out of the kitchen." I am not saying quit serving the Lord, but I am saying do not be surprised with people who will come against you and the attacks that you will receive, because that is part of the territory. Consider what Jesus experienced.

For consider him that endured such contradiction of sinners against himself, lest ye be wearied and faint in your minds.

(Hebrews 12:3)

Remember that, many are the afflictions (evil or adversity) of the righteous, but the Lord delivers you out of them "ALL." No weapon formed against you will prosper.

Many are the afflictions of the righteous: but the LORD delivereth him out of them all.

(Psalms 34:19)

No weapon that is formed against thee shall prosper; and every tongue that shall rise against thee in judgment thou shalt condemn. This is the heritage of the servants of the LORD, and their righteousness is of me, saith the LORD.

(Isaiah 54:17)

Jesus told us that in Him we have peace, but in the world we will have tribulation, but we are to be of good cheer, because He overcame the world.

These things I have spoken unto you, that in me ye might have peace. In the world ye shall have tribulation: but be of good cheer; I have overcome the world. (John 16:33)

Again we will endure suffering in the world, but peace in Jesus. Because Jesus overcame, we can also do it. Remember, we can do all things through Christ Jesus, who strengthens us. Jesus is our example for all things in this life.

I can do all things through Christ, which strengtheneth me. (Philippians 4:13)

Apostle Paul was an example of a man who really wanted to know Jesus Christ and His living and service to Him. *This should be the cry of all of our hearts.*

"That I may know him, and the power of his resurrection, and the fellowship of his sufferings, being made conformable unto his death;"

(Philippians 3:10)

Many times in today's world even many of those in the Body of Christ do not want to suffer pain in their service for Jesus Christ. If we truly desire to do the things that He did and live the way that He lived, suffering will be part of our service for Him. Remember, a servant is no greater than His master, if they persecuted Jesus, they will persecute us.

Remember the word that I said unto you, The servant is not greater than his lord. If they have persecuted me, they will also persecute you; if they have kept my saying, they will keep yours also. (John 15:20)

We need to thank God that when we suffer persecution, afflictions, and evil forces that come against us, we are a real threat to Satan and his followers. Remember to rejoice and be exceeding glad, for great is our reward.

Rejoice, and be exceeding glad: for great is your reward in heaven: for so persecuted they the prophets which were before you. (Matthew 5:12)

Suffering because of our relationship to Jesus Christ and obedience to God's Word is a positive and good thing, which really is beneficial for us in our walk with Jesus. We all should desire to grow and become more mature in the things of God.

For example: In the physical realm when we want to strengthen and build our bodies, we work out with weights, machines, and various things which bring resistance to our physical bodies. It may be painful, when we are doing our workout, but if we stay with it, we build and form our bodies to be strong, healthy and good-looking. We must go against resistance in our physical and spiritual bodies in order to grow and become stronger. When suffering for our faith in Jesus Christ, in reality, if we receive suffering with the right attitude, we grow and become stronger in Christ and are molded into His image in our character and actions.

Suffering for your faith in Jesus Christ and obedience to Him are major factors in your being molded into His image and reflecting Him to the world.

16

God's Purpose for His Grace

We hear the word "grace" said many times in the church world by many people, yet few really understand the true purpose, and that God gave us His Grace in spite of ourselves. Grace is: "unmerited favor, a gift, or something given that we did not earn." Because of God's Great Love for all mankind, He gave us His Love and Grace by sending Jesus to the cross for us, through Him we can born again, starting a new life with our sins forgiven, and provided everything pertaining to life and godliness. God extended His Love and Grace towards us, while we were yet sinners, Christ died for us.

According as his divine power hath given unto us all things that pertain unto life and godliness, through the knowledge of him that hath called us to glory and virtue. (2 Peter 1:3)

But God commendeth his love toward us, in that, while we were yet sinners, Christ died for us. (Romans 5:8)

God's "Unconditional Love" for us is what gave us His Grace "Unmerited Favor" in spite of ourselves. The psalmist said, "What is man that thou art mindful of him." This is the overwhelming question of how an All-Mighty and All-Powerful God shows us such mercy and grace. Like the hymn "Amazing Grace," it is truly amazing how God offers His Grace to all mankind. Talk about an offer that we cannot refuse,—sadly, many do, and live defeated, sick, poor, with no purpose in life, no joy and happiness, worried, fearful, stressed out with no peace.

What is man, that thou art mindful of him? And the son of man, that thou visitest him?

(Psalms 8:4)

It is by Grace that we are saved through faith in Jesus Christ. God offers us favor that we do not deserve to be forgiven and saved from going to hell, when we leave our physical bodies. God gave His Grace so we can be saved and go to heaven when we leave this earth. We can, as well, be whole in our spirit, soul and body, while on this earth, with every need met.

But my God shall supply all your need according to his riches in glory by Christ Jesus.

(Philippians 4:19)

If Jesus is our Shepherd, we will not want.

The LORD is my shepherd; I shall not want.

(Psalms 23:1)

When Jesus died on the cross and said, "It is finished:" He meant that the price was completely paid. All we have to do is receive Him as our Lord and Savior and believe His Promises to us to be complete, lacking nothing: spiritually, physically, financially, socially, mentally, or anything in our lives that is good.

119

When Jesus therefore had received the vinegar, he said, It is finished: and he bowed his head, and gave up the ghost. (John 19:30)

According as his divine power hath given unto us all things that pertain unto life and godliness, through the knowledge of him that hath called us to glory and virtue: (2 Peter 1:3)

We who are Christians live under God's Grace. By faith we have access to His Grace. God's Grace is upon us, but we must believe it by faith. By God's Grace we are enabled to do the things that Jesus did.

Verily, verily, I say unto you, He that believeth on me, the works that I do shall he do also; and greater works than these shall he do; because I go unto my Father. (John 14:12)

This is possible because Jesus lives in our hearts.

Ye are of God, little children, and have overcome them: because greater is he that is in you, than he that is in the world. (1John 4:4)

We must always be aware of Jesus within us to be able to accomplish, overcome, receive, be, and do what God's Word instructs us to do, and that we will accomplish the task through Him.

We live in a world in which we must produce and earn our way with no favor. If we do not produce, out we go. We think that we have to do things in our own strength and that no one will help us. We are used to making our own way, using our abilities, wisdom, and experience to make our decisions. This is the reason why many people struggle with God who gives us Grace that we did not earn and for whom we do not have to perform. God will give us all things if we will just receive His Son Jesus as Lord and Savior, and let Him lead our lives. Then we look at the things that God would have us do, which we cannot do in our own strength and ability, but think we must, not realizing that it is through Jesus Christ we can do all things.

I can do all things through Christ which strengtheneth me. (Philippians 4:13)

It is a matter of turning loose the helm of our ship, and letting God navigate our ship of life, and accomplish the supernatural and impossible things. It is then He will do through and for us in His strength. Remember, it is not by our power or might, we achieve success, but by His Spirit.

Then he answered and spake unto me, saying, This is the word of the LORD unto Zerubbabel, saying, Not by might, nor by power, but by my spirit, saith the LORD of hosts. (Zechariah 4:6)

The unmerited favor of God's Grace gives us access to everything in Heaven and the Power of God working in and through our lives. Some people would say that this statement sounds too good to be true. Well, God is not a man that He should lie.

God is not a man, that he should lie; neither the son of man, that he should repent: hath he said, and shall he not do it? or hath he spoken, and shall he not make it good? (Numbers 23:19)

We have this great treasure in our earthen vessels (bodies); believe it and act on it.

But we have this treasure in earthen vessels, that the excellency of the power may be of God, and not of us. (2 Corinthians 4:7)

121

The will and Desire of God for us as followers of Jesus is to do our best and what is right, following Jesus in obedience to Him and His Word.

There is therefore now no condemnation to them which are in Christ Jesus, who walk not after the flesh, but after the Spirit. (Romans 8:1)

In truth, as we follow Jesus in obedience to His Word, we will still fall short. We will never reach perfection in our earthly bodies, but we press towards the mark.

Brethren, I count not myself to have apprehended: but this one thing I do, forgetting those things which are behind, and reaching forth unto those things which are before. I press toward the mark for the prize of the high calling of God in Christ Jesus. (Philippians 3:13-14)

Where we miss the mark is where God's Grace is applied that covers all of our shortcomings and sins. The thing is, we need to be putting forth the effort to do what we are told by His Word. We cannot do nothing and say God's Grace covers us, even though we are doing wrong and do not put forth the effort to do right, but simply do our own thing. Do not abuse the Grace of God in your life.

Something else remains that we need to remember in the things of God: When you say I will try; you are preparing for failure and not accomplishing the task. You do not try, you do it. You must be determined to accomplish what you are called to do, because God will do it through you. The question is how can you not accomplish it when He is doing it? Is not God able to do all things? Nothing is impossible with

Him, therefore, nothing is impossible for you with Him doing it for you and through you.

Because of the Grace of God, He has a Plan and Purpose for your life. If you follow Jesus, you will have blessings, peace, and fulfillment in your life on this earth. You will also be rewarded in Heaven for your obedience and doing God's Word in your life.

For we must all appear before the judgment seat of Christ; that every one may receive the things done in his body, according to that he hath done, whether it be good or bad.

(2 Corinthians 5:10)

The world says you cannot have it both ways, but when you follow Jesus Christ, God's Grace brings you into everything in the Kingdom of God.

God's Grace to us should be a comfort that even though we do our very best and no matter how we fall short, He covers us with His Grace. We should learn from our mistakes that we become wise and do not make the same mistake twice. We grow through learning from our mistakes; nothing can happen in our lives that what Satan meant for evil, God still turns it around for good, if we let Him.

But as for you, ye thought evil against me; but God meant it unto good, to bring to pass, as it is this day, to save much people alive.

(Genesis 50:20)

17

Be Encouraged Not Weary in Well Doing

We are told in God's Word not to be weary in well-doing, because we will reap in coming seasons, if we do not faint or quit.

And let us not be weary in well doing: for in due season we shall reap, if we faint not.

(Galatians 6:9)

We are to count the costs before beginning anything, so that we will be able to finish a fulfilled life.

For which of you, intending to build a tower, sitteth not down first, and counteth the cost, whether he have sufficient to finish it?

(Luke 14:28)

To be victorious in our walk with Jesus, to please God, and be rewarded at the Judgment Seat of Christ, we must examine our motives behind all that we do. We must make sure that they are all done for God's Glory, not ours or for only personal gain, but to bring people to Jesus, help them to live a life pleasing to God and live in His Promises to them.

For we must all appear before the judgment seat of Christ; that every one may receive the things done in his body, according to that he hath done, whether it be good or bad.

(2 Corinthians 5:10)

In the Power of the Holy Spirit working through us, we are to pray for people to be set free from all the bondages of sin, sicknesses, poverty, and anything that prevents them from living a life of freedom in their spirit, soul, and body and, of course, serving Jesus Christ.

Verily, verily, I say unto you, He that believeth on me, the works that I do shall he do also; and greater works than these shall he do; because I go unto my Father. (John 14:12)

We have all been Commissioned and Commanded to bring people to Jesus Christ in the Great Commission.

Go ye therefore, and teach all nations, baptizing them in the name of the Father, and of the Son, and of the Holy Ghost: Teaching them to observe all things whatsoever I have commanded you: and, lo, I am with you alway, even unto the end of the world. Amen. (Matthew 28:19-20)

We must have the proper foundation and motives for our service and what we do to please and lift up Jesus to a lost and dying world, then we build on that foundation. When we do things for our own glory or with a selfish motive, God knows, because He examines our motives in all that we do.

All the ways of a man are clean in his own eyes; but the LORD weigheth the spirits.

(Proverbs 16:2)

When we live with the wrong motives, not only are we not rewarded, but we open the door for pride, fear, jealousy, rejection, strife, hate, and other evil actions of the flesh, to enter our lives. God is not part of our self-centered attitude. If our works are Scriptural, they will bring results. God's Word will not return to Him void. God honoring His Word through us in the gifts of the Holy Spirit to others does not mean that we are pleasing to God, but we are being used as a vessel to others. But remember, Satan will enter our minds with every evil work of the flesh. Our wrong motives do not only destroy us, but also others, and bring reproach upon the Gospel of the Lord Jesus Christ.

So shall my word be that goeth forth out of my mouth: it shall not return unto me void, but it shall accomplish that which I please, and it shall prosper in the thing whereto I sent it.

(Isaiah 55:11)

When you start out with the right motives, the next thing that Satan will do is try to tell you that you are insignificant, that what you do does not matter. He has you look at someone else, who is doing many great things and is recognized, and you feel small compared to these "perfect" humans. You must never compare yourself to others.

For we dare not make ourselves of the number, or compare ourselves with some that commend themselves: but they measuring themselves by themselves, and comparing themselves among themselves, are not wise.

(2 Corinthians 10:12)

God has a plan for each of us as individuals about what we are to do. We must find out what that plan is, do it to the best of our ability, and then trust God for the results. We will be rewarded for our obedience to God's Word and for the things that He wants us to do, not by our friends, husband, wife, or pastor, but each one of us as individuals.

Another area exists but is not being recognized by people who cause God's children to be discouraged. Something that we must establish is that God and only God rewards us. He can use people, but promotions, demotions or blessings come only from God. When we merit ourselves according to man's opinion of us instead of God's Word, then we are simply a man-pleaser and we are going to displease God. We will do what we think will please man and not consider what God's Word says about the issue.

Know that everything you do in the name of Jesus Christ for someone, you do unto the Lord. Whether it is a cup of cold water, drive them to the store, give them money, a smile for them, praying for them, a kind word, or whatever act of righteousness you do, God will reward you. The things you do for others are acts of righteousness (actions of a person in right standing with God). These actions should be a part of your everyday life and are good fruits that should accompany your Salvation.

Therefore if any man be in Christ, he is a new creature: old things are passed away; behold, all things are become new. (2 Corinthians 5:17)

We will reap from all of our acts of righteousness in the due season that God has appointed for us. These actions are sure things and God's promise to us, if we do not faint or give up.

And let us not be weary in well doing; for in due season we shall reap, if we faint not.

(Galatians 6:9)

Satan steals from God's children by getting them to quit, give up, and throw in the towel. Thus, we need to remain strong, knowing that God will reward us, not man. We are told to consider Jesus, the Author of our Faith, and His great suffering, so that we will not become weary and faint in our minds.

Looking unto Jesus the author and finisher of our faith; who for the joy that was set before him endured the cross, despising the shame, and is set down at the right hand of the throne of God. For consider him that endured such contradiction of sinners against himself, lest ye be wearied and faint in your minds. (Hebrews 12:2-3)

Remember, for 120 years Noah built the Ark. Other than the animals and wildlife, only eight people entered the Ark; Noah, his wife, their three sons and their wives.

But with thee will I establish my covenant; and thou shalt come into the ark, thou, and thy sons, and thy wife, and thy sons wives with thee.

(Genesis 6:18)

When Noah built the Ark, he was ridiculed, laughed at, and was unsuccessful in influencing any people to enter the Ark other than his family. He obeyed God for all those years, not stopping because of others not joining with him or ridiculing him for a 120-year period. Can you imagine that? Few people ever live that long, much less complete a project for God that lasted that long under difficult situations. At the end all on the Ark were spared, and everyone else died in the flood. This is a real example of well-doing and endurance, of not quitting.

The bottom line in your service for Jesus is to first: do it unto Jesus Christ for His Glory, to help people, and lead them to Him. Know that your rewards will come only from God and do not look to people. Do not compare yourself to others, in what they do and how they do it. Always do what you are called to do, forget about what others say, or think, and focus on what God wants you to do. In following these spiritual "rules," know that you are touching people for Jesus and that He will reward and promote you. Those that know their God will be strong and do mighty exploits.

And such as do wickedly against the covenant shall he corrupt by flatteries: but the people that do know their God shall be strong, and do exploits. (Daniel 11:32)

When we really get to know our God, He will use us mightily for His Glory; just ask Him.

18

Your Mind: The Beginning of Good or Evil

Our mind is the beginning place of good and evil that comes to us and is the battlefield. All of our battles are either won or lost in our minds. How we deal with our minds is critical, as it will determine the life we live on this earth and where we will spend eternity. We are to make our bodies living sacrifices unto God, and not be conformed to the world, but be transformed by the renewing of our minds.

I BESEECH you therefore, brethren, by the mercies of God, that ye present your bodies a living sacrifice, holy, acceptable unto God, which is your reasonable service. And be not conformed to this world: but be ye transformed by the renewing of your mind, that ye may prove what is that good, and acceptable, and perfect, will of God. (Romans 12:1-2)

We make every decision for our lives in our minds. Our minds must be renewed by the Word of God so that we will make godly and wise decisions. Unless our minds are renewed by

God's Word, we will not make the right decisions and will not believe and live by godly principles and will be unable to demonstrate Jesus Christ to a lost and dying world.

Our minds are like computers, so it is important what we put into them. What we put in our minds of the Word of God is what God brings back to our remembrance by the Holy Spirit in time of need.

But the Comforter, which is the Holy Ghost, whom the Father will send in my name, he shall teach you all things, and bring all things to your remembrance, whatsoever I have said unto you.

(John 14:26)

Some days when we read God's Word, we get many revelations that literally explode in our minds. Other times, however, we do not seem to get much. But remember, God's Word is going into our minds (computer). This feeding into our minds is profitable for us, so that the Holy Spirit can bring it back to our remembrance in our time of need. In truth, Bible reading and meditation are always profitable for us, whether we get many revelations or if it seems as if we are getting nothing from it. We must focus on not quitting whether we feel like it or not, and remember, we live by faith not by emotional feelings or carnal desires.

Everything we hear, see and the thoughts we have is processed in our minds. We must evaluate immediately all of our thoughts and determine if they are pure and godly or evil and negative. All of our thoughts we judge by God's Word; if they are contrary to the Word, we must cast them down immediately before they take root in our minds.

Casting down imaginations, and every high thing that exalteth itself against the knowledge of God, and bringing into captivity every thought to the obedience of Christ; (2 Corinthians 10:5)

One example of our relating to our minds is: Someone walks by us and does not speak. Right away we think: They don't like us, they're mad at us, they're ignoring us, or some other negative conclusion. The right thing to do would be to cast it down and forget it thinking that they might have been preoccupied or had something on their mind. If we are unable to accept this excuse, then we must approach them and ask them if they did not see us, usually that is the case, they just were preoccupied and did not see us. We must never dwell on things like that in our minds, or it will get to the point that we will develop a negative attitude towards that person.

In the first place we need to stop thinking the worst about people and any situation we see, but overlook with mercy and stop being so ready to believe the worst. I do not mean to overlook sin, but things that people do are not always the way we would do them, like personal preferences. If we always want to believe the worst, then we have a negative mind that needs to be renewed by God's Word. We need God to refill us with His Grace and Love so that we may give it to others. God's Love is shed abroad in our hearts. We need to give His Love to others and look at their potential, looking for the good and not focusing on the bad, the way that God looks at us. We need to embrace an attitude of love, and walk in love.

And hope maketh not ashamed; because the love of God is shed abroad in our hearts by the Holy Ghost which is given unto us. (Romans 5:5)

And walk in love, as Christ also hath loved us, and hath given himself for us an offering and a sacrifice to God for a sweet-smelling savour.

(Ephesians 5:2)

Never allow anything to remain in your mind that you do not want to become part of your life, for example: unforgiveness, hate, lust, judgment, jealousy, pride, wrath, and deception. The sooner you recognize these thoughts and cast them down in the name of Jesus, then you will have fewer problems and bad situations enter your life. Many thoughts will come into your life because of misunderstandings, poor communication with people, and being led away by your own lust. Sometimes Satan puts a thought into your mind to tempt you or downgrade you, and to make you want to give up. You will lose your joy and peace, if you allow these thoughts to take root in your mind. What you think on will become the most important thought in your life; it will enter your mind and overtake you. Remember, out of the abundance of your heart your mouth speaks.

O generation of vipers, how can ye, being evil, speak good things? For out of the abundance of the heart the mouth speaketh. (Matthew 12:34)

As you confess the negative things you begin to believe them and they become realities in your life. Faith comes by hearing, and hearing by the Word of God. As faith in God's Word and the confession of it bring godly positive results, your faith and confession in negative things brings negative, ungodly results.

So then faith cometh by hearing, and hearing by the word of God. (Romans 10:17)

A Spiritual Law that works for good or for evil. As a man thinks in his heart, so he is.

For as he thinketh in his heart, so is he: Eat and drink, saith he to thee; but his heart is not with thee. (Proverbs 23:7)

We are to think on honest, just, and true things.

Finally, brethren, whatsoever things are true, whatsoever things are honest, whatsoever things are just, whatsoever things are pure, whatsoever things are lovely, whatsoever things are of good report; if there be any virtue, and if there be any praise, think on these things. (Philippians 4:8)

An effort on our part is required to determine that we are not going to allow ungodliness, evil, and negative things to be parts of our mind. We need to ask God to help us discern good and evil thoughts by the Holy Spirit and the Word of God. It is a growing process, but we need to be practicing it in our lives 24/7; otherwise, it will not benefit us and we will suffer the consequences. We are to set our affections and minds on things above, not those on the earth.

Set you affection on things above, not on things on the earth. (Colossians 3:2)

God did not give us the spirit of fear, but of power, love, and a sound mind. We must have the mind of Christ.

For God hath not given us the spirit of fear; but

of power, and of love, and of a sound mind.
(2 Timothy 1:7)

For who hath known the mind of the Lord, that he may instruct him? But we have the mind of Christ. (1 Corinthians 2:16)

As we read and meditate on the Word of God, we receive wisdom, knowledge, and understanding from the Holy Spirit which enables us to know and be able to do things that are impossible for humans to do. God wants to do and accomplish the impossible through us so that He will be Glorified and Exalted. Jesus told each of us to believe that the things I do, so shall you do. Even greater things shall you do, for I go to my Father.

Verily, verily, I say unto you, He that believeth on me, the works that I do shall he do also; and greater works than these shall he do; because I go unto my Father. (John 14:12)

Live out of your spirit man not your human understanding and your five senses. We need to live our lives and serve the Lord out of our spirit and renewed mind, in order to accomplish what God's Word tells us.

Perfect peace is the result of our keeping our minds on Jesus Christ.

Thou wilt keep him in perfect peace, whose mind is stayed on thee: because he trusteth in thee. (Isaiah 26:3)

Peace and success are the results for our lives if we constantly meditate on God's Word.

This book of the law shall not depart out of thy mouth; but thou shalt meditate therein day and night, that thou mayest observe to do according to all that is written therein: for then thou shalt make thy way prosperous, and then thou shalt have good success. (Joshua 1:8)

We must be God-minded 24/7, if we are going to live out the Plan that God has for our lives. Being God-minded does not mean that we have a Bible in your hands all the time or on our knees praying 24/7. In truth, we are in the place that we hear from God, are sensitive to the Holy Spirit and are led by Him. He that dwells in the secret place of the Most high shall abide in the shadow of the Almighty. To dwell or dwelleth means to live there, "Live in the secret place of the Most High."

He that dwelleth in the secret place of the most High shall abide under the shadow of the Almighty. (Psalms 91:1)

Everything begins in our minds—our decisions, attitude, emotions, and thought processes. Our minds must be renewed by God's Word, otherwise we will think like our natural man or the way the world thinks.

And be not conformed to this world: but be transformed by the renewing of your mind, that ye may prove what is that good, and acceptable, and perfect, will of God. (Romans 12:2)

But the natural man receiveth not the things of the Spirit of God: for they are foolishness unto him: neither can he know them, because they are spiritually discerned. (1 Corinthians 2:14)

God's Word is Spiritual. Our minds must be renewed by the Holy Spirit to understand, be able to do, receive, be what we are instructed in His Word, and to be led by the Holy Spirit. When we are born again it is our spirit man, not our soul or body, we have to renew our mind (soul) by God's Word.

And if Christ be in you, the body is dead because of sin; but the Spirit is life because of righteousness. (Romans 8:10)

We, must live by our spirit man which is to be led by the Holy Spirit, with our mind (soul) in agreement with our spirit man, then walk it out in our body. Our spirit, soul, and body must live in agreement with one another. As God the Father, Son, and Holy Ghost are in perfect harmony and agreement, this is what we are to be. Example: We believe God's Word in our spirit man, our mind believes something else, and in our body we do something different from our spirit and soul. This is not unity and things will not work for us. We need to believe in our spirit man, think and believe the Word of God in our minds, and speak it out and do it in our bodies. We are 3 parts Spirit, Soul, and Body; they must be unified as one.

When it comes to our faith in God's Word we cannot be double minded, a double minded man is unstable in all his ways and will not receive anything from God.

For let not that man think that he shall receive any thing of the Lord. A double minded man is unstable in all his ways. (James 1:7-8)

We must learn to focus our minds on the Word of God and stand strong and fully persuaded that His Word is true and will do what it says it will do. The Bible tells us that strait is the gate and narrow is the way that leads to life.

Because strait is the gate, and narrow is the way, which leadeth unto life, and few there be that find it. (Matthew 7:14)

When we ask God in prayer for anything or claim His Promises to us, we must be single minded or use tunnel vision only, focused on what His Word promises us and making no room for failure, feelings, circumstances, what we or others think, or for a Plan B. We must be single-minded, fully persuaded that God's Word is All Truth, and that God means what He says and says what He means. If God's Word says it, that settles it!

In closing, God gave us a sound disciplined, well-balanced, and calm mind.

For God hath not given us the spirit of fear; but of power, and of love, and of a sound mind.

(2 Timothy 1:7)

We are to use our minds for what is good and beneficial to us and others according to God's Word and such use will bring Glory to our Lord Jesus Christ. Receive into your mind only the things of which Jesus would approve, because He knows what we are putting into our minds. Satan began his mind games and deception with Adam and Eve and they failed. Praise God for Jesus, who is the second Adam, and defeated him when He was led up by the Spirit into the wilderness to be tempted by the devil.

Then was Jesus led up of the Spirit into the wilderness to be tempted of the devil.

(Matthew 4:1)

If we make our bodies living sacrifices for Jesus to lead us by the Holy Spirit, we will overcome all worldly things, and fulfill God's Plan for our lives.

19

Stepping Out of Your Boat

A familiar passage of Scripture is where Jesus told Peter to "come out of" the boat to Him, and Peter walked on water to meet Jesus.

And Peter answered him and said, Lord, if it be thou, bid me come unto thee on the water. And he said, Come. And when Peter was come down out of the ship, he walked on the water, to go to Jesus. (Matthew 14:28-29)

Many times we fail to really understand what really took place during this event, in which Peter demonstrated great faith.

Today we all begin our relationships with Jesus in our own personal boats; this is in our infancy stages of being Babes in Christ. We all start out on the milk of God's Word and live on other people's faith, but there is a time, when God expects us to start becoming more mature in Him. Just as we when we had children, they were first babies, then toddlers, young children, teenagers, young adults, adults, middle-aged adults, then senior adults. This growth process happens as we grow in age. We would expect a child at the age of 12 to be at a certain level of maturity and not act like a baby.

God expects His children to mature with age and be at a certain maturity level. Yet, some Christians have been saved for 40 years and retain toddler maturity levels. In the natural a person would be retarded if they were 40 years old and acted like a two-year-old in their mentality. Yet, in the spiritual it is a common thing and not much is thought of or said about it. These people really do not understand about living by faith, things that we suffer for our stand for Jesus, the Promises of Jesus to us, and our Spiritual Authority over all evil and evil spirits.

Now the just shall live by faith: but if any man draw back, my soul shall have no pleasure in him. (Hebrews 10:38)

According as his divine power hath given unto us all things that pertain unto life and godliness, through the knowledge of him that hath called us to glory and virtue: Whereby are given unto us exceeding great and precious promises: that by these ye might be partakers of the divine nature, having escaped the corruption that is in the world through lust. (2 Peter 1:3-4)

Notwithstanding in this rejoice not, that the spirits are subject unto you; but rather rejoice, because your names are written in heaven.

(Luke 10:20)

And I will give unto thee the keys of the kingdom of heaven: and whatsoever thou shalt bind on earth shall be bound in heaven: and whatsoever thou shalt loose on earth shall be loosed in heaven. (Matthew 16:19)

Thus, we should study to show ourselves approved unto God and meditate on God's Word to be successful and victorious in our lives.

This book of the law shall not depart out of thy mouth; but thou shalt meditate therein day and night, that thou mayest observe to do according to all that is written therein: for then thou shalt make thy way prosperous, and then thou shalt have good success. (Joshua 1:8)

Many people look at God's Word as a history book about creation and what Jesus and the Apostles did when Jesus was on the earth. The Great Commission is an ongoing command to everyone born on this earth; we are a continuation of this command. Jesus said that we will do as He did on earth and that signs will follow us, if we believe.

Go ye therefore, and teach all nations, baptizing them in the name of the Father, and of the Son, and of the Holy Ghost: Teaching them to observe all things whatsoever I have commanded you: and, lo, I am with you alway, even unto the end of the world. Amen. (Matthew 28:19-20)

Verily, verily, I say unto you, He that believeth on me, the works that I do shall he do also; and greater works than these shall he do; because I go unto my Father. (John 14:12)

And he said unto them, Go ye into all the world, and preach the gospel to every creature. He that believeth and is baptized shall be saved; but he that believeth not shall be damned. And these signs shall follow them that believe; In my name shall they cast out devils; they shall speak with new tongues; They shall take up serpents; and if they drink any deadly thing, it shall not hurt them; they shall lay hands on the sick, and they shall recover. (Mark 16:15-18)

Today many people try to fit in their relationship with God in the midst of their busy lifestyles, worldly pleasures, and jobs trying to make money for things they want, as well as to build up a nest egg for what they think is security for themselves. These efforts are not wrong, but it is their priorities that people have wrong. We are to seek first the Kingdom of God, the foundation, and God will help you get your life in order in every area, He just wants to have first place in your life.

But seek ye first the kingdom of God, and his righteousness; and all these things shall be added unto you. (Matthew 6:33)

We live in a fast-paced world, but need to stop, let go, and let God manage our affairs and live according to God's Word, not our way or the way of the world. We must put God in the center of our lives.

Most Christians do not even consider their faith, authority, suffering, commission to service, and God's Promises, unless they have a great need. Then they come to God for help. We are to practice and apply God's Word to our lives 24/7 in all that we do. But if we live our lives the way the world does, except for going to church on Sunday and paying our tithes thinking that we are doing our duty to God, we are sadly mistaken.

But be ye doers of the word, and not hearers only, deceiving your own selves. (James 1:22)

Most Christians are still in their boat. Getting out of their boat means that they are daring to step out of their boats on God's Word and do what He wants them to do. To disregard the impossible but knowing God is a God of the impossible for them and going forward, knowing that is what He wants them to do, they will accomplish much in their lives in the name of Jesus Christ by the help of the Holy Spirit.

And he said, The things which are impossible with men are possible with God. (Luke 18:27)

Laziness, being worldly-minded, full of fear, lack of knowledge, wanting to stay in our comfort zone, innocent complacency, and trying to figure out how we will make it, are just a few of the reasons that keep us in our boats. We need to always be pressing forward to grow and improve in the things of God; otherwise we will become luke-warm and passive people.

I press toward the mark for the prize of the high calling of God in Christ Jesus.

(Philippians 3:14)

An example of continual going forward is like the hammer and ball game at a carnival or fair. We try to ring the bell, when we hit the pad with a big hammer. When the pad is hit, the ball rises, then when it stops whether it hits the bell or not, it starts coming back down from where it started. This game, in many ways, is like us. If we are not going forward, then we are going backward or backsliding. We know that we will never become perfect in our walk with Jesus in our bodies on this earth or ring the bell, but we keep improving, as we move forward.

Peter said, "Lord, if it is you bid me to come unto you on the water." As Jesus walked on the water, He told Peter to "Come" and he obeyed by getting out of the ship and walking on the water toward Jesus.

And he said, Come. And when Peter was come down out of the ship, he walked on the water, to go to Jesus. (Matthew 14:29)

This miracle shows that Peter so deeply believed Jesus that he was willing to do the impossible for all mankind and walk on the water. Stop right there and think about this miracle. If Jesus said, "Come," would you get out of a ship in deep water and start walking? Talk about the supernatural or impossibilities that is certainly one of them. You might say, "Yes, I would, if Jesus told me to do so."

Then why do people not tithe, when God's Word tells them to do so? Usually they say, "I don't have enough money to pay my bills, if I tithe. Is not God also able to take care of your bills? To us, His written Word is the same as His spoken Word. Read God's Word, and as you see and understand what He expects from you, obey Him without making excuses simply because your circumstances or situations are not right. Just do what God tells you.

He that observeth the wind shall not sow; and he that regardeth the clouds shall not reap.

(Ecclesiastes 11:4)

Moses made an excuse, because of his speech impediment.

And Moses said unto the LORD, O my Lord, I am not eloquent, neither heretofore, not since thou hast spoken unto thy servant: but I am slow of speech, and of a slow tongue. And the Lord said unto him, Who hath made man's mouth? or, who

145

maketh the dumb, or deaf, or the seeing, or the blind? have not I the LORD? Now therefore go, and I will be with thy mouth, and teach thee what thou shalt say. (Exodus 4:10-12)

Jeremiah made an excuse by saying he was too young.

Before I formed thee in the belly, I knew thee; and before thou camest forth out of the womb I sanctified thee, and I ordained thee a prophet unto the nations. Then said I, Ah, Lord God! Behold, I cannot speak: for I am a child. But the Lord said unto me, Say not, I am a child: for thou shalt go to all that I shall send thee, and whatsoever I command thee thou shalt speak.

(Jeremiah 1:5-7)

We must all recognize that when God tells us to do something, He not only commands us, but equips us and leads us to do the job through us. Often, the problem is that we plan to do the job in our wisdom and strength and realize that we are unable to do it, so we make excuses and stay in our boats. It requires us to use our faith in God's Word for us to accomplish things as well as to receive from Him. Remember, without faith it is impossible to please God.

But without faith it is impossible to please him; for he that cometh to God must believe that he is, and that he is a rewarder of them that diligently seek him. (Hebrews 11:6)

When Peter was walking on the water, he was allowing the wind, storm and the outside circumstances, which would be scary as he was walking on water, to distract him from Jesus and looked at the things that could stop or hurt him. But the bottom line is that if we keep our focus on Jesus and continue to keep on going and disregard all the negativity around us, we will surely reach the other side. Even though Peter took his eyes off Jesus, Jesus caught him and said, "O thou of little faith, wherefore didst thou doubt?"

And immediately Jesus stretched forth his hand, and caught him, and said unto him, O thou of little faith, wherefore didst thou doubt?

(Matthew 14:31)

Jesus was actually saying that He was with Peter, enabling him to walk on water, so how could he doubt Jesus because of circumstances? Are the circumstances that come against us greater than God and His Word to us? We must focus on Jesus and God's Word in all that we do.

Finally, to get out of our boat should be a one-time quality decision, and one with which we should remain consistent. But being realistic, there are times that we are weak in faith, tired, and lack motivation. We need to worship and praise the Lord, commune in prayer with Him, and meditate on His Word. I have found that during my more difficult times, if I offer a sacrifice of Praise and Worship to the Lord, I become renewed as if never being disconnected from Him in any way. Even though I was not disconnected from Him at those times, I experienced just a dry, empty feeling. The fact is that He says, "I will never leave you or forsake you."

Let your conversation be without covetousness; and be content with such things as ye have: for he hath said, I will never leave thee, nor forsake thee. (Hebrews 13:5)

Whatever a Truth or Fact, the emptiness and dryness are feelings. We walk by faith and not by sight.

(For we walk by faith, not by sight)

(2 Corinthians 5:7)

I have found that at times it seems like nothing much is happening for me. But actually those are the times when God is doing the most for me and getting things set up for greater things to come my way. Be encouraged in the quiet times and know that God is working on your behalf. Live your life out of your boat, and you will truly be reflecting Jesus to others.

20

Practice the Presence of Jesus in Your Life

I will never leave thee or forsake thee; this is a precious Truth and Promise of our Lord Jesus Christ to all of His followers. Truth we must always keep in our minds and hearts.

What a comfort to know that Jesus is in us to help and provide, to guide and protect. And Jesus gives us comfort and strength as we walk with him.

Ye are of God, little children, and have overcome them: because greater is he that is in you, than he that is in the world. (1 John 4:4)

No matter how we feel, our circumstances, our doing wrong, disobedience, or whatever our state, He will never leave us, but be there to help and lift us up. We need to make sure that Jesus' Presence is daily in our minds and hearts and we must never lose sight of this presence. If we do not know and practice this need, Satan will walk over us, intimidate, discourage, frighten us, steal from us, and cause us to give up. Jesus is our Shepherd, and we shall not lack or want in any area of our lives.

The LORD is my shepherd; I shall not want.

(Psalms 23:1)

Knowing that God Almighty is in us, and if God be for us, who can be against us?

What shall we then say to these things: If God be for us, who can be against us? (Romans 8:31)

In truth, as we are led by the Holy Spirit, we will never be defeated, and all things will work together for our good.

And we know that all things work together for good to them that love God, to them who are the called according to his purpose. (Romans 8:28)

We are to be bold and confident, as we follow Jesus. He will work in and through our lives, in His ability, not ours, so that we are never alone. Jesus is in us so He can reflect and demonstrate Himself in and through each of us; that God will be glorified. Jesus will never leave or forsake us.

Let your conversation be without covetousness; and be content with such things as ye have: for he hath said, I will never leave thee, nor forsake thee. (Hebrews 13:5)

If able to see into the spirit world, we could realize how we are really protected and supported by the Father, Son, and the Holy Spirit, and the multitudes of angels surrounding and protecting us. Elisha prayed that His servant would see in the spirit world what was really happening, when his servant was fearful of the men of Syria coming down to get Elisha, as they compassed the city. Elisha said that all of these persons who are with him (the spirit world) are more than they are with the Syrians.

150

God opened the servant's eyes and he saw the mountain full of horses and chariots of fire round about Elisha.

And he answered, Fear not: for they that be with us are more than they that be with them. And Elisha prayed, and said, LORD, I pray thee, open his eyes, that he may see. And the LORD opened the eyes of the young man; and he saw: and, behold, the mountain was full of horses and chariots of fire round about Elisha.

(2 Kings 6:16-17)

The conclusion was that Syria never came again into the land of Israel, God overcame the enemy.

And he prepared great provision for them: and when they had eaten and drunk, he sent them away, and they went to their master. So the bands of Syria came no more into the land of Israel. (2 Kings 6:23)

He that dwelleth in the secret place of the most High shall abide under the shadow of the Almighty. (Psalms 91:1)

This statement means that we are to live in the secret place of God for us, not just visit there from time to time or in our times of need. We will be under His Divine Protection, Provision, and Anointing for our ministry to others. As well, everything of which we have need will be supplied, that we might know Him and the Power of His Resurrection.

That I may know him, and the power of his resurrection, and the fellowship of his sufferings, being made conformable unto his death;

(Philippians 3:10)

To live the abundant life promised by Jesus is not only for our personal benefit, we will become more effective in the ministry that God has given us to help others while on this earth. To achieve this aim, we must develop an intimate relationship with the Lord through our commitment to Jesus, our faith, prayer, meditation in God's Word, worship and praise, and obedience to His Word. To be closer to Him should be our heart's desire, for God tells us to draw near to Him, and He will draw near to us. But we must make the initial effort to initiate the relationship.

Draw nigh to God, and he will draw nigh to you. Cleanse your hands, ye sinners; and purify your hearts, ye double-minded. (James 4:8)

When pleasing and living for Jesus Christ becomes your heart's desire, He will reveal Himself to you, and you will be conscious of His presence in your life. Others will also see Jesus in you, and you will effect a change everywhere you go, because you are anointed with His Power. This not only is for your personal benefit to live the abundant life promised by Jesus, but you will become effective in the ministry that God has given you to help others while on this earth.

The awareness of God's Presence with us will give us peace, boldness, confidence, and the secure knowledge that nothing can harm or defeat or get to us; they must go through God Almighty. We develop boldness, where we will do the things that a lot of people call risky, knowing that our Heavenly Father will meet that need, whatever it is. God's Word tells us that greater is He who is in us, than he is in the world. This is a true promise, but it becomes more of a reality and an effective truth for us and through us to others, if we dwell in the secret place of the Most High. The manifestation and affectivity of Jesus' Presence within us is when we are in the secret place of the Most High.

Ye are of God, little children, and have overcome them: because greater is he that is in you than he that is in the world. (1 John 4:4)

What we do not see with our physical eyes is far greater than the evil instruments Satan uses against us that we can see with our eyes. We must believe that God is fighting our battles and that through Him, we are more than conquerors.

Nay, in all these things we are more than conquerors through him that loved us.

(Romans 8:37)

No weapon formed against you will prosper. You never face anything by yourself; Jesus is always there to help, if you call on Him by His Word. He cares for your life, just as a mother hen does for her baby chicks; only far greater is His care for you.

No weapon that is formed against thee shall prosper; and every tongue that shall rise against thee in judgment thou shalt condemn. This is the heritage of the servants of the LORD, and their righteousness is of me, saith the LORD.

(Isaiah 54:17)

One of Satan's effective tools is to tell you that nobody cares about you, that you are all alone, you are the only one who is going through what you are experiencing, people always fail you and so does God. Satan tries to tell you to keep to yourself and stay away from people, because you do not need anyone. If Satan can get you alone and keep you that way, this is where he wants you in your life. He tries to divide and keep Christians by themselves, so that he can take advantage of them and cause many problems to destroy them. We need one another for support, counsel, prayer, and to help us fulfill our callings and ministry for Jesus Christ. In the multitude of counselors there is safety. We all are part of God's total picture for His Body.

Where no counsel is, the people fall: but in the multitude of counselors there is safety.

(Proverbs 11:14)

Divide and conquer is Satan's plan against Christians, because he knows there is power in numbers and in the unity of believers, because one will put a thousand to flight and two will put ten thousand to flight.

How should one chase a thousand, and two put ten thousand to flight, except their Rock had sold them, and the LORD had shut them up?

(Deuteronomy 32:30)

Our pity parties and "woe is me" are the tools used by Satan to keep us away from others. Our Constitution tells us that "United we stand, divided we fall." We all have a supply for the Body of Christ which is needful; being separated, we cannot make our supply, and the Body of Christ will be weakened.

But speaking the truth in love, may grow up into him in all things, which is the head, even Christ: From whom the whole body fitly joined together and compacted by that which every joint supplieth, according to the effectual working in the measure of every part, maketh increase of the body unto the edifying of itself in love.

(Ephesians 4:15-16)

To be more aware of God's Presence in our lives, we must Worship and Praise Him, pray and enter into His Presence, read and meditate in His Word. In following these pursuits, we will begin to know Him, and in knowing Him, we will know that He is always with us.

I talk to the Lord, and He talks to me. He gives me thoughts, speaks to my heart about things, offers answers to my problems, and gives me direction, guidance and wisdom. God gives me whatever is needed even when I am driving my car or watching TV. If you keep your spirit man open to God 24/7, you will fellowship with Him, and He will become more real to you. God is everywhere for and with you, so do not confine Him to certain places. I have seen miracles in stores, restaurants, amusement parks, and any place, where there are people.

In a wedding I performed years ago, they held the reception at a tavern in town. They asked me to join them, and just one other person and I went. The groom told me about how he respected me for accepting the invitation, because so many others turned up their noses at it. I went there with the intention of being a blessing to them, and God really used me to minister to the people. God anointed me, and I ministered to many men and women. I know that many seeds of God's love were sown as well as people touched by the Power of God. By the way, I drank a Coke—not beer or a mixed drink. I came out of that place, as blessed of God as I did after many church meetings.

Jesus went where they needed Him; the Pharisees accused Him of being with sinners and tax collectors and looked down on Him with their religious spirits. I do not say go to bars or taverns to minister, unless God leads you to do so, but if the occasion arises, do not miss an opportunity to share Jesus, if God leads you that way. Religion and religious spirits may come up against that sort of situation, but Jesus goes to heal, deliver, and set the captives free everywhere.

The mind and heart-sets you must establish are important. First of all, the Lord is with you all the time and everywhere you go. If you are doing wrong or at the wrong place, He will try to convince you to get out of there. If you are doing something wrong, He is there to lift you out of your sin. He will not leave or forsake you. These facts do not give you a license to sin or go to the wrong places, but Jesus is in you at all times. How you respond to Him is something different: You can obey or disobey Him, turn Him off and go your own way, or respond and obey Him. He knows your every thought, intention, action, reaction, in all that you do. If you try to fool God, you are a fool, who is simply fooling yourself.

The best way to experience the reality of God in your life is to obey His Word (the Bible). As you apply the scriptures to your life and follow them, you will see God perform them in and through your life. Some things happen instantly, others somewhat later, some over a greater period of time. Seeing God work in your life and through your life by ministering to others is what following Jesus is all about. But this seeing only happens, as you have faith in His Word, trust and obey Him, as He directs your steps.

The Bible tells us the things that God has written for us so that we who believe in Jesus Christ may know that we have eternal life.

These things have I written unto you that believe on the name of the Son of God; that ye may know that ye have eternal life, and that ye may believe on the name of the Son of God.

(1 John 5:13)

The Scriptures tell us, as I have declared in this chapter that Jesus will never leave or forsake us or cease to do the good work He has begun in our lives which He will continue to perform until we leave this earth.

Being confident of this very thing, that he which hath begun a good work in you will perform it until the day of Jesus Christ:

(Philippians 1:6)

21

Maintaining Motives in Spiritual Growth

We are told to press towards the "mark," which is the mark of perfection in Jesus Christ. We will never attain this mark on this earth, as Paul said that he did not apprehend it. But we must try to get increasingly closer to the mark as we grow in Jesus.

I press toward the mark for the prize of the high calling of God in Christ Jesus.

(Philippians 3:14)

In growing and going forward in Jesus Christ we are told that we must strive lawfully in order to be crowned or rewarded.

And if a man also strive for masteries, yet is he not crowned, except he strive lawfully.

(2 Timothy 2:5)

This is the area that shipwrecks many people, who want to grow and do mighty exploits in God.

And such as do wickedly against the covenant shall he corrupt by flatteries: but the people that do know their God shall be strong, and do exploits. (Daniel 11:32)

Our ambition can get in the way of God's will for us, because we try to accomplish the things we think necessary in the flesh.

You must make a quality decision, before really starting to effectively press towards the mark. This decision is: I will follow Jesus and be what He wants me to be, and do what He wants me to do, and not strive to be famous and noticed by men. Many think true success is being famous, and well-known; these can be attained, but if it is your motive, it is wrong. Your desire should be to be and do what God wants from you, and totally disregard where it will lead you. God will sometimes show you the vision, but recognize that there are often many steps, much learning and adult maturity that you need to have, until you arrive at that place. Do not be in a hurry. Just follow the leading of the Holy Spirit and know that you are in God's timing.

Knowing that we are at the place, where God wants us to be is the mark we need to maintain, if we are going to successfully press towards the mark of perfection in Jesus.

Brethren, I count not myself to have apprehended: but this one thing I do, forgetting those things which are behind, and reaching forth unto those things which are before, I press toward the mark for the prize of the high calling of God in Christ Jesus. (Philippians 3:13-14)

Such a mark of perfection alone should be to our complete satisfaction in reaching our goal, knowing that we are where we should be, and are pleasing to God; this is the most important thing in our effort, not where it leads.

God's ways and thoughts are not our ways and thoughts, but are above.

For my thoughts are not your thoughts, neither are your ways my ways, saith the LORD. For as the heavens are higher than the earth, so are my ways higher than your ways, and my thoughts than your thoughts. (Isaiah 55:8-9)

The Lord knows the doors to open for us, and also the doors to close. As well, He brings divine connections, as He has done for me. It has been this connection and an open door that have led me to write this book.

We can start out with the right motives in wanting to grow and become a mighty vessel in the hands of God. We must however, be very careful and not become impatient, and try to accomplish our goals in the flesh simply because things are not happening fast enough. Once we get into the flesh, then we will start doing things with the wrong motives. We will quickly sense our selfish will rising to do things only for our own gratification and interests. Remember, what is started in the Spirit cannot be completed in the flesh.

Pride is another area in our growth that can cause us problems. Watch when a man thinks he stands, because he could fall.

Wherefore let him that thinketh he standeth take heed lest he fall. (1 Corinthians 10:12)

Humility and the fear of the Lord (Respect and Reverence for God) are two attitudes we must have or we will fall into a dangerous attitude of self-pride. Pride is a major weapon of

Satan; remember, it was pride that caused him to be cast out of Heaven.

Thine heart was lifted up because of thy beauty, thou hast corrupted thy wisdom by reason of thy brightness: I will cast thee to the ground, I will lay thee before kings, that they may behold thee. (Ezekiel 28:17)

Ambition is good, if it is in obedience of God's leading in our lives, and not a selfish motive in which we will do anything necessary to accomplish our goals, like striving unlawfully (according to God's laws). Ambition is only good when it is based on a godly foundation; otherwise, many go to excessive means to fulfill their ambitions.

All that we do should be: For the Glory of God and in the name of Jesus Christ, and to help others and bring them to Jesus. That is the only motivation for which we will be rewarded at the Judgment Seat of Christ.

Every man's work shall be made manifest: for the day shall declare it, because it shall be revealed by fire; and the fire shall try every man's work of what sort it is. If any man's work abide which he hath built thereupon, he shall receive a reward. If any man's work shall be burned, he shall suffer loss: but he himself shall be saved; yet so as by fire.

(1Corinthians 3:13-15)

It is not by our power or might, but by the Spirit of God that aids us to accomplish all things.

Then he answered and spake unto me, saying, This is the word of the LORD unto Zerubbabel, saying, Not by might, nor by power, but by my spirit, saith the LORD of hosts. (Zechariah 4:6)

Jesus told us that without Him, we can do nothing.

I am the vine, ye are the branches: He that abideth in me, and I in him, the same bringeth forth much fruit: for without me ye can do nothing. (John 15:5)

We will eventually come to recognize that our human efforts will not get the job done and understand that our weapons are not carnal, but mighty through God to the pulling down of strongholds. It is then that we will learn to walk our Christian Life in the Power of God using our faith in His Word, speaking His Word, and becoming an overcomer in all that we face in life.

(For the weapons of our warfare are not carnal, but mighty through God to the pulling down of strong holds; (2 Corinthians 10:4)

When we walk in a life of victory and see His Hand upon us, working in and through us to others, we must recognize that it is not just our own efforts, but that it is by His Mercy and Grace in our lives that He enables us by His Power to accomplish the tasks that He leads us to do and also receive the Promises that He has given us through Jesus Christ, and the shedding of His Blood. Every good thing in our lives is only given by God's Grace and Mercy through Jesus Christ. Give God all the glory and praise and make known His deeds to the people.

O GIVE thanks unto the LORD; call upon his name: make known his deeds among the people.
(Psalms 105:1)

In conclusion, our lives and growth in Christ are considered a race. It is not how fast we run the race, but about running the race lawfully (by God's Laws) with patience, and finishing the race. Jesus is our example of the one who finished His race, lawfully, with the right motives and patience. We are always to consider Jesus in all that we do. If we follow His example, we will always do right and have the endurance to finish our race. Our problem may be that we do not always follow Jesus as our example. Remember, always follow Jesus.

WHEREFORE seeing we also are compassed about with so great a cloud of witnesses, let us lay aside every weight, and the sin which doth so easily beset us, and let us run with patience the race that is set before us, Looking unto Jesus the author and finisher of our faith; who for the joy that was set before him endured the cross, despising the shame, and is set down at the right hand of the throne of God. For consider him that endured such contradiction of sinners against himself, lest ye be wearied and faint in your minds. (Hebrews 12:1-3)

22

God's Chastisement for Us

The word "chastisement" means in Greek "tutorage or education of training; by implication disciplinary correction; chastisement or chastening, instruction or nurture." Many times these are thought of as negative actions, when people are chastened by God; but it is just the opposite, when we submit to it in our lives. All Christians are to be chastened by God, and if we are not, then we are bastards and not sons.

But if ye be without chastisement, whereof all are partakers, then are ye bastards, and not sons. (Hebrews 12:8)

We would surely agree that none of us have hit the mark or are perfect in our walk with Jesus. In the physical we know it is painful to develop a muscular and well-toned body. This development takes a lot of work, commitment, and determination with which we must stick, until we receive the intended results and then maintain those results.

Somehow in the spiritual or our spirit man we do not understand that the same spiritual law is involved. We think suffering and pain are wrong in our spirit man, but the bottom line is that we must stretch our faith, our tolerance level, our self-discipline, and other areas of our spirit man, if we want to be a strong, muscular, and well-toned spirit man, like we do to achieve a strong physical body. Applying God's Word to our lives, tests, using our faith, dealing with opposition, and being treated unfairly are just a few things that will either cause us to get bitter or better—our choice. Consider Jesus and how He experienced the maximum of everything, while He was on this earth.

Furthermore we have had fathers of our flesh which corrected us, and we gave them reverence: shall we not much rather be in subjection unto the Father of spirits, and live? (Hebrews 12:9)

We are not to despise the chastening of the Lord, or faint when He chastens us. Whom the Lord loves, He chastens. If we endure the chastening, God will deal with us like sons.

And ye have forgotten the exhortation which speaketh unto you as unto children, My son, despise not thou the chastening of the Lord, nor faint when thou art rebuked of him: For whom the Lord loveth he chasteneth, and scourgeth every son whom he receiveth. If ye endure chastening, God dealeth with you as with sons; for what son is he whom the father chasteneth not? (Hebrews 12:5-7)

The Chastisement of the Lord is neither a pleasant thing nor is working out strenuously pleasant. But the results that come from chastisement are well worth the effort.

Now no chastening for the present seemeth to be joyous, but grievous: nevertheless afterward it yieldeth the peaceable fruit of righteousness unto them which are exercised thereby.

(Hebrews 12:11)

If we faint or quit, when chastened by God, then we miss the teaching and training and will never reach a level of maturity as a Christian. If we yield to the chastisement and learn from it, we will receive the peaceable fruit of righteousness.

If we want to grow and mature in the Lord when we are chastened by God, it is all about our attitude and the way we approach things in our lives. It is for our good, so we must submit to it, and not quit or faint.

If a person gives you a hard time at your workplace, they say bad things about you and treat you terribly, you become angry with them. God speaks to your heart and tells you to tell them: "If I've offended you in any way, forgive me, and I also forgive you for anything that you've done to me." That would be the work of a peacemaker, I have offered forgiveness before, and as I know many of you have. It is the Lord correcting you and telling you the right thing to do. It is hard to do sometimes, but you need to ask God to help you do it. Remember, you can gain much strength if you will work with and through Christ Jesus.

I can do all things through Christ which strengtheneth me. (Philippians 4:13)

Corrie Ten Boom, a Dutch Christian who helped the Jewish people escape the Holocaust during World War Two with her sister and father, were all captured and sent to a concentration camp. Her father and sister died in the camp, but she was later released, because of a clerical error that God used to set her free. She forgave the most cruel and evil prison guards, who hurt her and her family and caused the death of her family. We must bless those who do evil to us and forgive those who have offended us.

Bless them which persecute you: bless, and curse not. (Romans 12:14)

And when ye stand praying, forgive, if ye have aught against any: that your Father also which is in heaven may forgive you your trespasses. But if ye do not forgive, neither will your Father which is in heaven forgive your trespasses.

(Mark 11:25-26)

This is an extreme example, not a normal situation for most Christians. But remember, God is trying to mold us into the image of His Son, a task which demands us to reckon ourselves dead to sin and alive to God.

Likewise reckon ye also yourselves to be dead indeed unto sin, but alive unto God through Jesus Christ our Lord. (Romans 6:11)

Dying to our selfish desires and yielding to God's Will for our lives are painful processes. The pain and suffering we experience is the dying of our selfish will in doing God's Will. Some people think sickness, disease, physical suffering, poverty, and accidents are what God brings on us to teach us a lesson; this is wrong. These things Jesus Christ bore and paid for on the Cross for us by His Blood. These are curses, and Jesus redeemed us from the Curse of the Law.

Christ hath redeemed us from the curse of the law, being made a curse for us: for it is written, Cursed is every one that hangeth on a tree:

(Galatians 3:13)

If someone should accuse you of bringing these terrible things into your child's life to teach them a lesson, you would be offended and would probably be ready to fight. Do not accuse God of putting something on people that is from darkness and in Satan's domain. God speaks to your heart, telling you to do right and follow His Word. When you determine to walk in the Word of God and in His Love, then that is where the battle begins with self, Satan, the world, and even many times with those close to you. When you are betrayed by those you love, you become hurt and angry which are normal emotions. But the quicker you go to God and ask His help to forgive and pray for the people who hurt you, and then your situation becomes better.

We all have feelings, as Jesus did; Jesus wept. We are not dehumanized as Christians, but are to use and obey God's Word in all situations, not our emotions and feelings, no matter how justifiable they may be. We will either listen to our human nature or obey God's Word, which in all things is the complete opposite of our human nature.

Jesus wept. (John 11:35)

But the natural man receiveth not the things of the Spirit of God: for they are foolishness unto him: neither can he know them, because they are spiritually discerned. (1 Corinthians 2:14)

It is only by the help of the Holy Spirit that we can accomplish things the way God wants by His Word. To try to accomplish the things that God tells us with our own abilities is as ridiculous as we trying to lift up a Cadillac automobile above our heads. If we wanted to do that, we would put it on a hydraulic lift, hit the button, and it would go above our head. Father God in the name of Jesus Christ is our Hydraulic Lift for all things. Just hit His button in the name of Jesus Christ, and it works 24/7.

If we want to be more like Jesus, it will be painful and will cost. When we tell God that we want to be more like His Son Jesus, we are really saying: Heavenly Father I want to live less in my human nature and more in the God Nature of your Son Jesus. God then begins to direct us in the way that we will obey His Word and not our human nature and selfish will. We need to be cleansed from our human nature by God chastening and filling us with the Holy Spirit. Remember, the suffering is well worth it, for the great rewards that the effort yields.

For I reckon that the sufferings of this present time are not worthy to be compared with the glory which shall be revealed in us. (Romans 8:18)

23

Having Sure Faith with Patience Produces Results

A problem that causes many Christians to become disheartened and discouraged is because they do not see and experience an answer to their prayers, after releasing their faith. Hopes (expectation) delayed makes hearts sick.

Hope deferred maketh the heart sick: but when the desire cometh, it is a tree of life.

(Proverbs 13:12)

We must know that having met God's conditions brings assurance that we have the result, whether having received the manifestation immediately or not. I wish to explain in this chapter the approach that needs to be taken when we pray, so that we can be assured of answers to our prayers. I have found this approach to be effective, because it is according to God's Word and brings results.

First of all, we need to find the scriptures that pertain to the need we have.

And this is the confidence that we have in him, that, if we ask any thing according to his will, he heareth us: And if we know that he hear us, whatsoever we ask, we know that we have the petitions that we desired of him.

(1 John 5:14-15)

Secondly, we need to make sure that there is no sin or unforgiveness in our hearts and lives.

If I regard iniquity in my heart, the Lord will not hear me: (Psalms 66:18)

We must ask the Lord by the Holy Spirit to examine our hearts and lives and reveal to us what we need to do for any corrections. When our request comes from our hearts, He will show us anything we need to stop doing, start doing, or changes to be made. Repent, make things right, and live with a clean heart.

Create in me a clean heart, O God; and renew a right spirit within me. (Psalms 51:10)

The chapter on "Unforgiveness," deals with the issue of unforgiveness. If you are having a problem in this area of your life, refer to that chapter. When you have made sure of these two areas, then you need to keep free from sin and unforgiveness. If you sin, you need to ask God's forgiveness immediately, receive it, and forgive yourself and go forward.

If we confess our sins, he is faithful and just to forgive us our sins, and to cleanse us from all unrighteousness. (1John 1:9)

The key is dealing with both sin and unforgiveness, which is also a sin, and when you see it in your life, deal with it immediately! Ask the Lord to make you sensitive to the Holy Spirit in every area of your life, because if you gain this sensitivity, He will let you know when you are about to take a wrong step, or you will sense in your heart a prompting from Him, when you do wrong or sin.

The steps of a good man are ordered by the LORD: and he delighteth in his way.

(Psalms 37:23)

Thirdly, control your thoughts regarding for what you are standing in faith, as well as all things that are not according to God's Word. Cast down these thoughts in the name of Jesus Christ, as they come into your mind.

Casting down imaginations, and every high thing that exalteth itself against the knowledge of God, and bringing into captivity every thought to the obedience of Christ; (2 Corinthians 10:5)

All negative thoughts should be cast down and you should not think about or dwell on them. When you dwell on them, it will take hold of you and cause you to see the problem bigger than God, and Satan will steal from you the things you believe.

The thief cometh not, but for to steal, and to kill, and to destroy: I am come that they might have life, and that they might have it more abundantly. (John 10:10)

Remember, Satan is trying to steal all that God has promised us; he uses our natural senses and gives us negative thoughts to try to accomplish this. We have the Word of God, the Holy Spirit, the Name of Jesus, the Blood of Jesus, the Angels, and all of Heaven behind us to stop him, but we must see it, act upon Satan's evils, and not allow him to steal from us. This situation is like the old saying, "You cannot stop birds from flying over your head, but you can stop them from landing on it."

Fourth, we have to control our tongue; death and life are in the power of the tongue.

Death and life are in the power of the tongue: and they that love it shall eat the fruit thereof.

(Proverbs 18:21)

In order to follow all these conditions, we need to fill our minds with God's Word, especially the word regarding for what we are standing in faith. We need to confess the scriptures out loud, and call it done in Jesus name. Remember, God called the things that be not as though they were.

For verily I say unto you, That whosoever shall say unto this mountain, Be thou removed, and be thou cast into the sea; and shall not doubt in his heart, but shall believe that those things which he saith shall come to pass; he shall have whatsoever he saith. (Mark 11:23)

(As it is written, I have made thee a father of many nations,) before him whom he believed, even God, who quickeneth the dead, and calleth those things which be not as though they were.

(Romans 4:17)

When we speak negative words about what we believe, we can negate or stop our prayers from bringing forth results, because we get what we believe and say. Out of the abundance of our hearts our mouths speak, so that is why it is so important to be full of God's Word and speak only His Word regarding all things in our lives.

A good man out of the good treasure of his heart bringeth forth that which is good; and an evil man out of the evil treasure of his heart

bringeth forth that which is evil: for of the abundance of the heart his mouth speaketh.
(Luke 6:45)

Speaking of the good in life is the creative force God used in creating the world. He said: "Let there be light" or "Light Be".

And God said, Let there be light: and there was light. (Genesis 1:3)

God spoke the world into existence. Watch your words and be slow to speak carefully.

Wherefore, my beloved brethren, let every man be swift to hear, slow to speak, slow to wrath:
(James 1:19)

Fifth, see your prayer request manifest from the spiritual realm into the physical realm and act like you have the answer. Faith believes you have what you believe, whether the result of your request manifests immediately or not.

Therefore I say unto you, What things soever ye desire, when ye pray, believe that ye receive them, and ye shall have them. (Mark 11:24)

What you can see with the eyes of faith, you can have true faith. Continually thank and praise God for the results after you release your faith for the result or answer.

Sixth, is the area where most people quit or give up, because the desired results do not manifest quickly enough for them, and they get tired of waiting, or think their prayer was not answered. They give up their faith and lose the answer to their prayers. When things do not manifest immediately, they must apply the Spiritual force of Patience which is the twin of Faith which will ensure the manifestation, when it does not manifest immediately.

But let patience have her perfect work, that ye may be perfect and entire, wanting nothing.

(James 1:4)

After we have found the word that covers our request from God and ensure that our hearts are right, then release our faith. If the manifestation does not appear immediately, then apply Patience, which is simply believing, saying, and acting like we have the answer and standing firm until it manifests, keeping all our words positive and full of faith. When praying we must determine to stand, until our request manifests, not moved by what we feel, see, hear, but what God's Word says about our request. When we get to that place in our faith, we will not have to stand very long, until it manifests. In our faith we must be determined, fully persuaded, and know that we have our answer, and we will have it.

Cast not away therefore your confidence, which hath great recompense of reward. For ye have need of patience, that, after ye have done the will of God, ye might receive the promise.

(Hebrews 10:35-36)

In closing, this is our confidence. If we ask anything according to His Word, God hears us, and if we know that He hears us, then we know that we have the desired petitions of Him! It is really that simple.

And this is the confidence that we have in him, that, if we ask any thing according to his will, he heareth us: And if we know that he hear us, whatsoever we ask, we know that we have the petitions that we desired of him.

(1 John 5:14-15)

24

Walking in God's Timing is Not an Option

To every thing there is a season, and a time to every purpose under the heaven:

(Ecclesiastes 3:1)

Being in the time or timing can make the difference between success and failure. I am reminded of trapeze artists, and how their timing must be precise or it could result in tragedy. When a person lets loose of the bar, swinging far above the ground, just as that person is falling, the catcher must be there to catch them, they must meet at the exact second or the person will fall.

When it comes to the things of God, we must also be in His timing or it will not work. I share with you two examples in my life of success and failure by being in God's timing for success and being out of His timing, resulting in failure.

The first event was years ago, when a lady called me. Both she and her husband were friends of my wife and me. An older man lived as a boarder in the home of my friend's mother, who was on his death bed in a coma. I was asked to come to the mother's home to minister to the elderly man. It was around suppertime when my friend called, and I was busy that night, so I decided to put calling her off until the next day. God used my wife to tell me that I needed to go that night and not wait until tomorrow. So I went and spoke to him even though he was in a coma. By the way, people still hear you, even when they are in a coma, and so you must always speak faith-filled words of encouragement. After speaking to him, I led him in prayer and gave him time to respond, even though he could not vocally respond to me. When finished, the mother and her daughter asked me: How will we know what happened? Good question. So we prayed and asked God to give us a sign, and then I left.

The next day I had a call from the lady. Two things had happened that I never forgot and were valuable lessons that I learned. First of all was timing. The man died around 6:00 a.m. that morning, so if I had waited until the next day, it would have been too late, I thank God that He used my wife to keep me from making a major wrong decision that would have made the difference of a man going to hell instead of Heaven. The next thing that happened I am sure you guessed, God gave us a sign that the man was saved that night and went to Heaven. Life and death could be in your timing. Always let God lead you. When He says jump, you say, "How high?" then do it. You will know by the Holy Spirit if it is a now or later thing. What I am saying is do it when you are told and forget about the "what-if's."

My second testimony cost me something, because I did it my way. One day years ago, a crown popped off my tooth. I put the crown in a tissue and in a drawer, then made a dental appointment to have it recemented. I got up the next day forgetting that I had put the crown in the tissue and tossed it in the trash basket. Meantime, I was looking for my crown, but could not find it. I went to work and a little after lunch, the Holy Spirit reminded me of what I did. He enlightened me and I felt relieved, because I then remembered that I put it in the trash can.

About one hour until break-time I realized I could finish my job quota for the day, but only if I stayed on the job until break-time. The Lord impressed upon me to go now, call my wife and tell her that the crown was in the trash basket. But I thought: What difference would one hour make? I'll finish my job, and then do it. Well, at break-time I called my wife to tell her about where the crown was. She said, "Oh no! I just emptied the baskets of burnable items, put them in the 55-gallon drum, and burned it just minutes ago."

Looks like that hour I thought did not matter cost me a crown for my tooth, of about $400 worth, years ago when they were much cheaper. God knew what was going to happen and tried to warn me, but I thought to do it my way, which cost me money. I did it my way, but I believe Father God knew best.

Having read my two testimonies, I think you can understand the importance of doing what God tells you to do with no questions asked. Really when you do not do something when God tells you to do it, but decide to wait until later, that is an act of disobedience.

If you want God to lead you in all things, first of all you cannot lean to your own understanding.

Trust in the LORD with all thine heart; and lean not unto thine own understanding.

(Proverbs 3:5)

God knows all things, and we see things dimly, so we are not qualified to make decisions that will guarantee us a positive result. This is the reason we always need God's wisdom in our lives. We must always ask Him, and be led by the Holy Spirit on what, how, and when to do whatever He has us to do.

If any of you lack wisdom, let him ask of God, that giveth to all men liberally, and upbraideth not; and it shall be given him. (James 1:5)

Knowledge is to know something. Wisdom is to know how and when to apply our knowledge to any situation. To put it simply, God knows everything, while we outside of God only operate by sight, circumstances, past experiences, and feelings which generally lead us to failure. Does it not make sense to be led by someone who has all the answers?

Jesus used farming, seeds, and crops as His examples for us to learn spiritual laws and how to cooperate with them for results. We must sow seeds before reaping a harvest. Farmers must plant and grow crops before they can harvest them. There is a time to sow and a time to reap.

While the earth remaineth, seedtime and harvest, and cold and heat, and summer and winter, and day and night shall not cease.

(Genesis 8:22)

When God set the stars, sun, moon, planets, and the world, He had them in a certain order and timing that if they got out of order or timing, many would run into one another and crash. God purposely set these entities in precise order and timing to function as we see them today.

The Bible is full of the timing of God; we labor 6 days and rest on the 7th day, 50 days from the resurrection of Jesus until the day of Pentecost. Joshua was told to march around the wall of Jericho with his army once every day for 6 days and on the 7th day he was to march around 7 times. Noah was told by God to build an Ark by the specifications that He gave him. Solomon was told and instructed by God to build the Temple. God has a time and a way for us to fulfill His plans for us, as we serve Him. We must do exactly what He wants us to do and when He wants us to do it. Remember God's ways and thoughts are not ours. Unless we follow His leading and timing, we will miss the mark.

For my thoughts are not your thoughts, neither are your ways my ways, saith the LORD. For as the heavens are higher than the earth, so are my ways higher than your ways, and my thoughts than your thoughts. (Isaiah 55:8-9)

Our old nature is past when we come to the Lord. Now we have a new nature that wants us to do what it wants, as well as when it wants to do it. We must be careful that we do not fall into the trap and do things when we want or we will miss the mark every time.

When we choose to pick the time, we do things because of the circumstances or for it to fit into our schedule. Even though God is telling us to do it now, we are doomed to failure. We must learn that God's timing is perfect and anything else will not work.

Procrastination is a bad habit. Many people know to do something, but put it off until a later date or many times do not do it. It is sin, when we know to do the right thing and do not do it.

Therefore to him that knoweth to do good and doeth it not, to him it is sin. (James 4:17)

In closing, our old nature is to do things that we want to do, and when we want to do them. Many times we do not have time to do something, but I have found that including myself and others, if we really want to do something, we will make time for it. Also in the same mode, if we really believe God's way is the only and right way, we will obey Him by making the effort to do what He tells us and when He tells us. We will never reach perfection in this life. We can, however, get closer to it by working toward receiving the high calling offered by God in Christ Jesus.

I press toward the mark for the prize of the high calling of God in Christ Jesus.

(Philippians 3:14)

25

Our Mission: Finish What Jesus Started

Jesus started the ministry that He wanted His church to continue doing on earth, after He returned to Heaven to sit at the right hand of the Father.

If ye then be risen with Christ, seek those things which are above, where Christ sitteth on the right hand of God. (Colossians 3:1)

Jesus demonstrated and taught His Apostles how and what He wanted them to do, as the first Church (Body of Christ) came into existence. Jesus gave us the Great Commission and told us to do what He did, while He was here on earth.

Go ye therefore, and teach all nations, baptizing them in the name of the Father, and of the Son, and of the Holy Ghost: Teaching them to observe all things whatsoever I have commanded you: and, lo, I am with you alway, even unto the end of the world. Amen. (Matthew 28:19-20)

Verily, verily, I say unto you, He that believeth on me, the works that I do shall he do also; and greater works than these shall he do; because I go unto my Father. (John 14:12)

We first must recognize the fact that in all we do on this earth that it is not in our power, but that of the Holy Spirit. We cannot do anything without Jesus.

Then he answered and spake unto me, saying, This is the word of the Lord unto Zerubbabel, saying, Not by might, nor by power, but by my spirit, saith the LORD of hosts. (Zechariah 4:6)

I am the vine, ye are the branches: He that abideth in me, and I in him, the same bringeth forth much fruit; for without me ye can do nothing. (John 15:5)

The Body of Christ has been given the Great Commission and empowered to accomplish everything that Jesus did while here on earth. God neither tells us to do something that we cannot do, nor gives us an assignment that we cannot accomplish. We can accomplish all things through Jesus Christ.

I can do all things through Christ which strengtheneth me. (Philippians 4:13)

It is up to us whether we do what God's Word tells us to do and be obedient to the Holy Spirit, or do what we want to do. The choice is ours. Unless we are a doer of God's Word, we will not be fruitful vessels.

But be ye doers of the word, and not hearers only, deceiving your own selves. (James 1:22)

God tells us to do things that we in ourselves cannot accomplish, but only through Jesus and by His help can it be done. The reason for this is so that we will have to trust Him and have faith in His Word and not ourselves. Then others will know that it was God who did it; no man will receive the glory for it, as only God will get the Glory and Honor due to Him.

We can do everything that Jesus did while on earth, except what He did on the Cross. For others to see Jesus Christ in our lives there are two areas that we must consider. The first area is what people saw, when they were around Him—His character, the type of man He was, and His ability, which was the mighty power which He demonstrated to the people. I will first explain character, the foundation of all that we do. Without good character; we bring reproach to the Gospel of Jesus Christ as well as reflect a bad testimony. All that He showed in His character was in the Fruit of the Spirit, which are in us; our job is to use them in every area of our lives and not give into our carnal nature. The Fruit of the Spirit will help us know our new man in Jesus.

But the fruit of the Spirit is love, joy, peace, longsuffering, gentleness, goodness, faith, Meekness, temperance: against such there is no law. (Galatians 5:22-23)

Therefore if any man be in Christ, he is a new creature: old things are passed away; behold, all things are become new. (2 Corinthians 5:17)

For example: Love is one of the fruits. When people hurt us or become our enemies, while we want to hurt them or get even, God says to love them.

But I say unto you, Love your enemies, bless them that curse you, do good to them that hate you, and pray for them which despitefully use you, and persecute you; (Matthew 5:44)

We must choose to exercise God's fruit of love in us over our selfish will, desires, or feelings. Longsuffering is another fruit that needs to be exercised, when we want to give up and quit because of circumstances. When we ask God to help us and determine in ourselves not to give up or quit, we exercise the fruit of long-suffering in our lives.

Jesus' character was the Fruit of the Spirit. Exercising the fruits in our lives is not easy and can only be accomplished through the Power of the Holy Spirit within us. Our part in exercising the fruits is to lay aside our will and feelings and determine to do it God's way. Then it will happen, but only when we come to the place that we are determined to work according to God's Word no matter what we feel or think. Only then will God help us to overcome that obstacle and reflect to others Jesus in us. To overcome an obstacle is dying to self, and living for God.

Likewise reckon ye also yourselves to be dead indeed unto sin, but alive unto God through Jesus Christ our Lord. (Romans 6:11)

While I have named just two of the fruits in us, I think you understand what I am trying to show you regarding the denying of our selfish wills and doing what is asked of us God's way. Demonstrating God's fruits will reflect our character to others and please God, because they see His way demonstrated in our lives.

Now that we have explained what Jesus' character was and how to establish our character to be like that of Jesus through the Fruit of the Spirit, we are ready to look at the other side of Jesus—His ability, which was in the Gifts of the Spirit.

But the manifestation of the Spirit is given to every man to profit withal. For to one is given by the Spirit the word of wisdom; to another the word of knowledge by the same Spirit; To another faith by the same Spirit; to another the gifts of healing by the same Spirit; To another the working of miracles; to another prophecy; to another discerning of spirits; to another divers kinds of tongues; to another the interpretation of tongues: But all these worketh that one and the selfsame Spirit, dividing to every man severally as he will. For as the body is one, and hath many members, and all the members of that one body, being many, are one body; so also is Christ. (1 Corinthians 12:7-12) Everything Jesus did was through the Gifts of the Spirit: Healing the sick, knowing the future, raising the dead, casting out demons, having wisdom and discernment; all were within the Gifts of the Spirit.

If Jesus would have demonstrated His character and ability in His God form, we could say that we are not God and naturally cannot accomplish it. God purposely had Jesus live as a man on earth to show this character through the Fruit of the Spirit that He has given within us to use. His ability was demonstrated through the Gifts of the Spirit, which the Holy Spirit demonstrates through us, as He wills.

By God having Jesus live on earth, we can do everything that Jesus did, because we have access to His gifts. But it is up to us to deny ourselves, obey and allow the Fruit of the Spirit to operate in our lives. We must be open and ask God to use His Gifts of the Spirit through us, as they are needed to help people, as Jesus did.

Our character is first most important as a foundation. Without good character people will have little respect for us and we will be unable to influence or bring them to Christ. Bad character brings only reproach. Developing good character is painful and not a glamorous task; it is about dying to self and our feelings and submitting to God's way. Was this submission not what Jesus did? He denied Himself and became poor, that we can become rich.

For ye know the grace of our Lord Jesus Christ, that, though he was rich, yet for your sakes he became poor, that ye through his poverty might be rich. (2 Corinthians 8:9)

This denial does not mean that He was poor on earth; it means that being in Heaven's Splendor with streets of gold and gates of valuable stones, unexplainable riches, the greatest wealth on this earth compared to Heaven, which is poverty. Jesus at Gethsemane also said that the Father's Will be done and not His, regarding Jesus' Crucifixion that lay ahead.

And he went a little farther, and fell on his face, and prayed, saying, O my Father, if it be possible, let this cup pass from me: nevertheless not as I will, but as thou wilt. (Matthew 26:39)

Jesus was always obedient and in the Perfect Will of the Father at all times. We know in our bodies that we will never walk a perfect walk, as

Jesus did. But we must press towards that mark and do our best to obey the Word of God and to live a life that reflects Jesus Christ and one pleasing to God.

I press toward the mark for the prize of the high calling of God in Christ Jesus.

(Philippians 3:14)

In closing, the message that I have tried to convey is that we have been called, commanded, anointed, and equipped to do the things that Jesus did while on earth. He was here for only 33 years and His ministry lasted for a little over 3 years. He died, was buried, resurrected, and returned to the Father. It is our calling and duty to demonstrate Jesus Christ to a lost and dying world, until His very, very soon return which He will take us home to Heaven.

After this I looked, and, behold, a door was opened in heaven: and the first voice which I heard was as it were of a trumpet talking with me; which said, Come up hither, and I will shew thee things which must be hereafter.

(Revelation 4:1)

God's Will was that it all began with Jesus and was to continue after He left earth and commanded the work for His Body to accomplish and fulfill. Remember, you are living and ministering to others in God's strength and power, not yours, therefore, expect God's results in and through your life, so that He may be glorified in and through you.

26

Personal Relationships Affect Your Heavenly Relationship with God

The relationships you have on this earth will affect your relationship with God. There is an old anonymous saying: "Be careful of the company you keep."

Be not deceived: evil communications corrupt good manners. (1 Corinthians 15:33)

We are not to have a friendship with angry-spirited people.

Make not friendship with an angry man; and with a furious man thou shalt not go: Lest thou learn his ways, and get a snare to thy soul.

(Proverbs 22:24-25)

We tend to develop the attitudes and ways of people with whom we have a personal relationship, whether good or bad. It is easy to do the wrong thing, which is why it is so dangerous to be around people who are ungodly and not of good character.

God's Word tells us that we are not to have a relationship with one who is not a true believer.

Be ye not unequally yoked together with unbelievers: for what fellowship hath righteousness with unrighteousness? And what communion hath light with darkness?

(2 Corinthians 6:14)

God's Word tells us that we should not date, marry, go into business with, have a personal friendship with, or link ourselves in any way to unbelievers, as far as being connected, where we could be influenced by them. We are to be friendly and kind to them and be witnesses to them, but not form a best-friends relationship. In truth, if we are truly letting our lights shine for Jesus to those that are lost around us, they will either try to get away from us, or will show us an interest that they are being influenced by our testimony for Jesus, and we can possibly lead them to Christ.

Many times Christians become involved with unsaved, unprincipled or ungodly people and do not let their lights shine or show Jesus to them. Wanting to fit in, they compromise their principles to be accepted. If we really love the Lord Jesus and His Word, how can we feel comfortable around those people in a fellowship relationship?

And have no fellowship with the unfruitful works of darkness, but rather reprove them.

(Ephesians 5:11)

People who are not saved cannot understand why you say and do the things you do; it makes no sense to them, as they are carnally-minded.

But the natural man receiveth not the things of the Spirit of God: for they are foolishness unto him: neither can he know them, because they are spiritually discerned. (1 Corinthians 2:14)

The people with whom we need to surround ourselves are those people that lift us up and not put us down. Friends are supposed to add to us, not take away. A true friend has our best interest at heart, will tell us the truth about ourselves, even if it hurts. A good acid test with people including Christians is: How do we feel or what type of spirit do we sense after talking to them on the phone or spending time with them face-to-face? Are we lifted up, encouraged, instructed, or helped in any way? If we are brought down in spirit after being with them, then we need to realize that they are pulling us down and that is not good for us. If they encourage us, and we feel or sense a good spirit, then that is good for us.

Always consider what our relationships are doing for or against us in our lives. If we realize a relationship is bad, then we need to get away from that person or if good, then it is alright. We do not realize and wonder sometimes why we are negative, short-tempered, or feeling depressed. These feelings could mean that is the spirit or attitude of those with whom we surround ourselves.

For teenagers and young people following God's Word is a much more difficult thing to do. One way to aid our young people is to begin in the home with the parents, teaching and showing Jesus to their children and grounding them in God's Word and godly principles. Thus they will be fully equipped to face the world. If they know that their home is a safe place, a refuge and a place for help and healing, then they will have somewhere and someone to turn to. As a support our churches need to have strong youth-group leaders and groups that deal with life as it is today to guide, direct, love and encourage our young people.

A bad thing that is overlooked many times is a saved girl or boy dating someone who is not saved. Sounds innocent, but this is a case where principles are compromised and people get hurt. Some in today's society and its people think premarital sex is alright; the truth is that it is not, but is a sin.

Marriage is honourable in all, and the bed undefiled: but whoremongers and adulterers God will judge. (Hebrews 13:4)

Our youth are being taught that premarital sex is alright, so if the girl is saved and the boy is not, usually he will pressure her and cause her to compromise her principles, or visa versa. This is the reason there now exists an epidemic of teen pregnancies.

Many Christians do not know the truths in God's Word and bring a lot of bad situations to the public scene, not just to the unsaved. We need to study and learn God's Word, so that we do not sin against Him.

Study to shew thyself approved unto God, a workman that needeth not to be ashamed, rightly dividing the word of truth. (2 Timothy 2:15)

Thy word have I hid in mine heart, that I might not sin against thee. (Psalms 119:11)

How many times have you seen or heard of both young and old people who were Christians, then got in with the wrong crowd and went back into the world? This type of misfortune should tell you that you should not join up and fellowship with people who are not saved, or even saved people, who have judgmental attitudes, hate, are full of unforgiveness, are racists, prideful, complainers, hold negative attitudes, or enjoy controlling people. If you are serving the Lord, these characteristics will make you uncomfortable around these kinds of people; keep away from them.

Winning people to Jesus is not simply becoming close friends with them; it is showing them that you love and care for them in showing Jesus to them by your actions and words.

Behold, I send you forth as sheep in the midst of wolves; be ye therefore wise as serpents, and harmless as doves. (Matthew 10:16)

We are not to be like the world. We want them to be like us as followers of Jesus Christ.

And be not conformed to this world: but be ye transformed by the renewing of your mind, that ye may prove what is that good, and acceptable, and perfect, will of God. (Romans 12:2)

We are set apart from the world as Christians. In truth, we are a royal priesthood on this earth.

Sanctify them through thy truth: thy word is truth. (John 17:17)

The Lord knoweth how to deliver the godly out of temptations, and to reserve the unjust unto the day of judgment to be punished: (1 Peter 2:9)

If you are not married, ask God to send you the mate that He has for you and let God be the one who approves of your future mate. Ask God to send the people to you that He wants to also be your friends and business partners, those with whom you can develop a good, healthy relationship, which will be for the betterment of all involved.

Remember your relationships on earth affect your relationship with God. Surround yourself with godly and successful friends, who have proven God's Word in their lives and can be a positive influence on your life.

27

God Has a Personal Plan for Your Life

God the Father sent His Son Jesus to die on the Cross for all mankind, but we need to remember that He is also a personal God. He created many species of flowers, animals, birds, fish—and the list goes on. Each species is individual. For example, the flower has its own particular identity; the rose is not like the lily or carnation; a robin is not the same as an eagle. We are all human beings, but not one of us has a duplicate. Even with twins, close as they are in appearance, there is always something different about one—their personality, a facial feature or a special habit. We are an original, and God has an original plan just for our lives.

For I know the thoughts that I think toward you, saith the LORD, thoughts of peace, and not of evil, to give you an expected end.

(Jeremiah 29:11)

God has a personal plan for every person on this earth; a plan for what God has created them and called them to do. We were all created by God for a purpose in this life. The first step is making Jesus Christ Savior and Lord of our lives, and then walking obediently to Him, as He leads us in our lives' journeys. Living our lives in God's plan for us is what we are called to do.

It is this area with which the Christians have a problem. We have a tendency to think that we know what God wants us to do, then take it to God and ask Him to bless what we are about to do. In the first place we need to ask God what His Plan is for our lives and let Him direct and bless His Plan for us. When we step out before knowing what God wants for us, it will not work. We can ask God to bless it, but He only blesses His Plan for us, and not ours.

Another important fact is when God speaks to your heart about doing something, unless it is clear and not full of doubts, you need to ask Him how you are to go about it. For instance: God tells you that He has called you into the ministry. You do not just run out there to preach. You receive the call and ask, "Lord, what is the next step in my calling?" Maybe it is Bible School or just shutting yourself in, so that God can speak to you. Do not always assume that you will be a pastor or an evangelist. You could be a youth leader, a teacher, author, writer, and so on.

There are many steps to our calling and much necessary preparation, especially to serve in the five-fold ministry.

And he gave some, apostles; and some, prophets; and some, evangelists; and some, pastors and teachers; For the perfecting of the saints, for the work of the ministry, for the edifying of the body of Christ:

(Ephesians 4:11-12)

We must be spiritually mature, which only comes from faith and obedience to God's Word by trials, tribulations, and persecutions that happen to try our faith.

Beloved, think it not strange concerning the fiery trial which is to try you, as though some strange thing happened unto you: (1 Peter 4:12)

We live in a microwave and instant world, but the things of God take time and faithfulness to prove ourselves and become mature and ready for our calling.

I THEREFORE, the prisoner of the Lord, beseech you that ye walk worthy of the vocation wherewith ye are called. (Ephesians 4:1)

Abraham waited 25 years until Isaac was born, when he finally became father of many nations that God had promised him. David also waited 25 years, until he became leader over all Israel, as God had promised him. I do not say that you will wait 25 years, but there are steps that will lead you to your destination. Only God can lead you, but you must follow Him to get there. Be patient, and learn while you are going to your destination with God, for that is His Plan for everyone—be patient and learn.

In February 2012 God opened a door for me to write this book, even though I have never even dreamed about writing a book. I was ordained into the ministry in 1975. After all these years of ministry, pastoring, evangelizing, and mostly everything in ministry, here I am writing this book. But I had 37 years as a five-fold minister

(Ephesians 4:11), as well as 5 former years, in which I served God in other areas of the church. God is using my knowledge and experience through many hard times, such as believing in God for your next meal. I have learned how to trust and believe God's Word and how to please Him, so now I am writing this book to help the five-fold ministry as well as non-five-fold ministers. Everyone is a minister, to live, show, and share the Gospel of Jesus Christ to those with whom they come in contact.

God has given you talents and giftings

So we, being many, are one body in Christ, and every one members one of another.

(Romans 12:5)

Your talents may be special things that you can do, such as sing, be a good speaker, have compassion for the elderly and ability to work with young people. These are giftings and talents that God can use through you for others in various areas of ministry. Learn for what you have ability, ask God to cultivate it, and use that ability for His Glory through you. To learn the ability and talents in your life you must ask yourself: What do I enjoy doing? Am I good at it? Does it bring positive results? This is one of the ways that you discover some of the things that God can do through you.

When God tells you to do something, always remember, He never asks you to do anything for which He does not equip you and will see you through to accomplish it. You will complete it successfully, if you follow Him and let Him direct you. Remember, you can do all things through Jesus Christ.

I can do all things through Christ which strengtheneth me. (Philippians 4:13)

Use the talents and giftings that God gave you for the purpose of you using them in the Plan that He has for your life. Do not be envious or jealous of someone else's abilities. Do what you are to do, because you are rewarded on your faithfulness to the Plan that God has for your life, not the size of the Plan. Remember, to whom much is given, much is required.

Not getting into God's Plan for our lives is the area that causes us not to receive the blessings and promises that He has given us through His Son Jesus Christ. Unless we put Jesus first in our lives, let Him be Lord and direct us in the way that He wants us to go, we will not live abundant lives.

But seek ye first the kingdom of God, and his righteousness; and all these things shall be added unto you. (Matthew 6:33)

This is where many Christians are in their lives today, with nothing happening and no results in their lives from prayer, because they are not asking God for His Plan for them. They are not allowing Him to direct them in His Plan for them. Remember, all these things are added to us after we first seek God's Kingdom.

We can only live and stay in God's perfect peace by our obedience to Him in fulfilling His Plan in our lives. God's Plan is for us to allow Him to fulfill it in us, then His Plan is to bless us in every area of our lives above our wildest dreams on earth, reward us at the judgment seat of Christ, and at the end tell us: "Well done, thou good and faithful servant."

For we must all appear before the judgment seat of Christ; that every one may receive the things done in his body, according to that he hath done, whether it be good or bad.

(2 Corinthians 5:10)

28

Miracles

A miracle by definition is an event or action that apparently contradicts known scientific laws such as the miracles in the Bible.

Accounts of numerous miracles appear in the Old Testament that were performed by God through many of His prophets and men such as Moses, Elijah, Elisha, and others. In the New Testament Jesus performed His first miracle on earth at the wedding feast of Cana, where He turned the water into wine.

This beginning of miracles did Jesus in Cana of Galilee, and manifested forth his glory; and his disciples believed on him. (John 2:11)

Miracles will continue, as long as there are human beings on this earth. God shows Himself through miracles as well as ministering to our needs many times in that way. God is a supernatural God, not limited by our natural laws such as the law of gravity. He made all of the laws and can supercede them or the impossibilities of mankind, as He wills. God can do above our wildest dreams and imaginations according to His Word, if we dare to have faith in Him to do it.

I will share with you some special miracles experienced in my life in service for Jesus Christ. These are miracles the Lord has done in my life and ministry.

A number of years ago my wife and I and family traveled to Heritage USA from our Maryland home during the Christmas holiday. My wife and I were staying at a lodging there at the time. One evening while walking on the grounds, I saw an older lady and a few other ladies sitting on the hotel steps. The ladies appeared as if something was happening to her; she was bent over, seemingly feeling sick. My wife and I went over to her and the ladies and discovered that she was having a heart attack. God told me to take hold of her hands and pray for her, and when I did, she immediately sat up and appeared all right.

On that cold night we took her up to her room, where she was staying and laid her on the bed. But she would not move her hands loose from mine, but firmly held on.

The hotel personnel had called for medical help, who came into the room shortly thereafter. But it was only after they prepared to take her to the hospital that she finally turned my hands loose from hers.

God's power flowed into her and she did not appear to need help, but they insisted on taking her to the hospital to be examined.

The ladies told me that she was from Canada and was in her late seventies. I gave them my address, so I could find out her outcome. A few weeks later she sent me a letter that she was having tests, but was fine. God instantly stopped a heart attack, which I had never seen happen before and had healed her.

Another time I was in a service at my home church, where that evening we had an invited guest speaker. A lady with a little girl who had a bad case of club feet asked me to pray for her daughter before the service. I felt it best not to pray then, but told her that we would pray after the service during the prayer time for the sick. I was not the pastor there and had no part in the service, being there only for the evening service.

During the call for the sick, God had me go forward and placed me before the people, the pastor, and the guest evangelist. God had me do something that I had never before done: I told everyone that they should not touch the little girl, unless they could believe that the Lord would immediately straighten the little girl's feet before our eyes.

The pastor stepped back as well as some of the people. The altar was surrounded by many people, but none came near her. I laid my hands on her feet and the guest evangelist put his hands on my shoulder. Before I prayed, Satan said to me, "You fool. You will be humiliated after you pray, because nothing is going to happen." Well, I prayed and others, at least the evangelist, agreed with me. God straightened both of her club feet and they became normal before our eyes. Praise God for His faithfulness.

A number of years ago my neighbor's two sons were in an automobile accident, while traveling at high speed. Their grandmother called and asked me to go to the hospital and pray for them, so I went that afternoon. When I entered their room, I did not recognize the one brother, because his face was distorted, swollen, mangled and he was in a coma. I did recognize his brother who was in the same room, so I knew it was him. I prayed for both boys, one in a coma and the other out of it, being heavily sedated for pain.

That evening, a few hours after I had prayed for the boys, their mother called me to report that her son had come out of the coma after several days. About an hour later she called me back to tell me that he was to be put into a regular room out of intensive care.

About a week later the boy who came out of the coma was sent home, his face completely healed and normal. The other son was sent home shortly thereafter. Jesus the healer was on the scene for the two boys. Glory to God!

Another miracle, quite different from most I had ever experienced was when my wife's grandmother was in the hospital suffering from hardening of the arteries. She was not able to recognize her children, because of her loss of mental faculties. My wife and I went into her room, but she really did not know who we were. However, we prayed and ministered to her, and all of a sudden the room literally lit up with a great light shining over the entire room. This great light lasted for a short period of time, then ceased. We led her to the Lord that night, a miracle, because she was over 80 years old at the time.

Later, she always asked about my wife, her granddaughter, and how my ministry was doing. Her interest in our family clearly showed my wife and me that God had touched her heart in a special way and that is why she remembered us. We were a link between her and God—not us, but the Lord through us. I was only her granddaughter's husband and for her to ask about my ministry and church was completely out of character for her until that time.

Whenever people touch our lives we can forget them, but no matter in what shape our mind is, when God touches our hearts, we will never forget it. She never forgot us and always asked about us until her death. God did a special thing for her by opening up her heart, saving her soul, and revealing Himself to her in a special way.

I have also seen over the years God do miracles in dogs numerous times, because He loves our pets. Anything that is important to us is also important to Him. God wants us to care for animals and our pets, as they are also important to Him.

A righteous man regardeth the life of his beast: but the tender mercies of the wicked are cruel. (Proverbs 12:10)

I wish to share with you two of these miracles about the love God has for animals. A number of years ago my parents had a Schnauzer called Pepper, because his fur was the color of pepper. He became sick and progressively got worse. After a few days he turned a yellowish color like a yellow jaundice and did not eat or move around, he just laid there. I did not know what the sickness was, but knew that he was very sick. I went over one evening after I got the critical news to pray for him and he looked like he was almost gone, with no reaction in him. I laid hands on him and prayed, and nothing appeared to happen in the natural at that time, so I left about 15 minutes after I prayed for him.

My family and I lived about 20 miles from my parents. On my way home, the Lord told me that he was healed. This had happened about 10 minutes after I left, so I was really anxious to get home to call my parents. At home my wife told me that my father had called and told her that Pepper was healed, was back to normal. And that beloved dog never had a sick day after that.

I asked my wife what time my dad called and discovered that it was the same time that God told me that Pepper was healed. We all thanked and praised the Lord for His love, mercy and grace towards us and for healing and sparing an important member of our family.

Another miracle that God performed was when my wife and I and family returned home from church after a mid-week church service. When pulling into our driveway, I saw a big dog (I believe she was an Iris Setter) lying on the side of the driveway. When I went over to the dog, blood was coming out of her mouth and other areas of her head. Her owner's son came over, saw the dog and said that it was too late. I did not accept that opinion. I prayed over the dog, and then I asked the family if I could take him to the vets and for the son to go along with me.

We put the dog in the back of the vehicle and took him to the vet. While on the way I continued to pray, and it seemed like she kept getting stronger and starting to show life. Every mile we traveled, she just got better and better. After we arrived at the vet's, I was really confident about what I saw going on in the dog, but the vet said she had only a 50/50 chance, but I knew the dog was healed. This was about 10:00 p.m.

Well, the next day I learned that the crisis was over. The vet called my neighbor and told him to pick up their dog. About 4:00 p.m. I saw them come home. The dog jumped out of the vehicle, ran over and jumped up and kissed his owner. It looked like nothing had been wrong with her. The time frame was approximately 19 hours from the time she was lying in my driveway. But with God nothing is hopeless. Most people would have given up at the sight of her injuries, but my God came through and made her whole. There is nothing that God cannot do.

Another miracle, for which I will be eternally grateful, happened to my wife. My wife and a friend going shopping one afternoon were about to turn into a shopping area and did not see another vehicle coming in the far lane in front of the store entrance. They made their turn, when suddenly a car came out of nowhere, sped in the lane and hit their vehicle broadside on the passenger's side, where my wife was seated.

Before the impact my wife yelled "Jesus!" She later said that she did not really feel anything after the crash, but was unable to get out of the car because the door was crushed and jammed. The emergency crew had to use the jaws-of-life to get her out. The next thing, where she sat was a sharp piece of glass aimed toward the jugular vein in her neck. Her friend saw it and warned her about the glass piece, so that she would not turn her head; otherwise, the glass would have cut into her jugular vein.

They took her to the hospital and only discovered some bruises, so basically she was fine. The police officer told my wife that just a few days before, there was an accident identical to the one she was in and the lady died that was seated in the exact same place where my wife had been on the passenger's side.

A few days later I went to look at the automobile. I looked at the seat where my wife had sat, and the door had jagged sharp metal aimed on the inside towards my wife's seat. On the left side of my wife was a console between her and the door. There were only inches of space there, less than one foot of space which in the natural to look at it, she should have had the metal door's sharp edges run into her right side, which were like knives pointing toward her.

I almost fainted upon seeing those sharp edges, because there was absolutely no possible way that she would not have been killed, except by God's angels who protected her and saved her life. Thank God for His mercy and grace for sparing my wife's life. This was a situation that could not be explained, and was impossible to figure out. My God is the God of the impossible. I just know that God somehow did it through Jesus Christ, my Lord and Savior. Even though

I do not understand or know how He saved my wife's life, I thank God and Praise Him for doing what my family felt was the impossible.

But Jesus beheld them, and said unto them, With men this is impossible; but with God all things are possible. (Matthew 19:26)

When I worked for a loan company several years ago, one particular time there was a lady who came into my office for a loan. As we talked, I discovered that she wanted the money for an abortion. Well, I started to minister to her regarding abortion and after I finished, she still got the loan, but not for an abortion. She told me there were other places to go for her loan, but she just knew that she had to come to the place I worked at that time. She also told me that she knew, as soon as she came into my office, that she was not going to have the abortion. Thank God that He directed and corrected her, so that she did not have the abortion.

I felt good about that meeting, but it was nothing compared to what I saw about five years later. One afternoon this same woman came into my office with a beautiful little girl, and guess what? It was the little girl who God stopped her mother from aborting five years earlier. It was a wonderful experience to see the beautiful little girl who almost became another statistic of aborted babies. When you see something like that, you never forget it. Where would we be without God intervening in our lives and giving us miracles?

I often think of many miracles that God has done for my wife and me. There are many times we recall when our lives were spared. None of us know how much in totality that God has done for each of us by providing for our needs and protecting us from harm. We will not know all the answers, until we leave this earth. Thank God for miracles.

Another miracle involved a man in his eighties who lived with the parents of a couple who were and still are close friends of mine. The man was in a coma, when I was asked to go to the home where he was staying and pray for him. I went into the home, where my friend's mother lived, and she was there with her daughter. The man in a coma was hard-of-hearing, and was known to be a mean person. I went over to him, prayed and shared the gospel with him, as if he was wide awake and listening to me. I gave him the opportunity to receive Jesus Christ as Lord and Savior, and then led him in the sinner's prayer. When I finished ministering to the man, the ladies asked me how we would know what happened after I ministered to him. I prayed and asked the Lord to show us, and shortly thereafter I went home.

The next morning the lady called and told me that the man had died sometime about 6:00 a.m. God had answered my prayer for Him to show us what happened the night before, so we would know if he received Jesus as his Lord and Savior, God confirmed that miracle to us. Every morning his covers were messed up and in array, but that morning were neatly in place, which showed us that God's peace was in him. Another part of the miracle was that he was in his eighties. Statistics show that fewer people receive Christ at that age. As well, he was hard of hearing and could not have heard me at the volume I spoke to him. He was in a coma, but God went through all of that and saved him only eight or nine hours before his death.

A word for anyone who visits someone in a coma: Their spirit can hear you; that is the reason why you must be careful about what you say, because they know. Speak only God's Word and uplifting words in their presence, and nothing negative. Lift them up by the Word of God, and use your faith on their behalf.

29

Heaven to Gain and Hell to Shun

This last chapter of my book is the foundation on which this entire book is based as well as the foundation of God's Word (The Bible). First of all, hell was not created for mankind.

Then shall he say also unto them on the left hand, Depart from me, ye cursed, into everlasting fire, prepared for the devil and his angels:

(Matthew 25:41)

Even though hell was not created for mankind, if our names are not written in the Lamb's Book of Life, we will be cast into the Lake of Fire. It is essential for readers to know that the Lake of Fire is the final destination for eternity to those that are without Jesus Christ.

And whosoever was not found written in the book of life was cast into the lake of fire.

(Revelation 20:15)

Hell is where unsaved people go, when they die without Jesus Christ as their Savior. To better understand, it is like a person on earth who commits a crime, and are put in the local jail to await trial and if found guilty in their trial, they are sent to the penitentiary. Hell is compared to the local jail, and the Lake of Fire is compared to the penitentiary. Before going to the penitentiary, they have a trial first, and before people are cast into the Lake of Fire, the Great White Throne Judgment must take place.

And I saw a great white throne, and him that sat on it, from whose face the earth and the heaven fled away; and there was found no place for them. And I saw the dead, small and great, stand before God; and the books were opened: and another book was opened, which is the book of life: and the dead were judged out of those things which were written in the books, according to their works. And the sea gave up the dead which were in it; and death and hell delivered up the dead which were in them: and they were judged every man according to their works. And death and hell were cast into the lake of fire. This is the second death. And whosoever was not found written in the book of life was cast into the lake of fire. (Revelation 20:11-15)

People who are now in hell and those who go to hell will remain there until the Great White Throne Judgment. It is then that their bodies will come out of the graves and reunite with their spirit and soul, which come up out of hell and stand before God. Here, they are judged, then cast into the Lake of Fire. This happens immediately before the new heaven, new earth and the New Jerusalem.

AND I saw a new heaven and a new earth: for the first heaven and the first earth were passed away; and there was no more sea. And I John saw the holy city, new Jerusalem, coming down from God out of heaven, prepared as a bride adorned for her husband. (Revelation 21:1-2)

Hell is located below, somewhere in the center of the earth.

The way of life is above to the wise, that he may depart from hell beneath. (Proverbs 15:24)

It is the place where people go who die and are not born again in Jesus Christ. It is a place that is eternal (never-ending). Those sentenced to go there will be given a body that will never completely burn, even though it will be in fire. The body will be similar to that of the burning bush that Moses saw.

Where their worm dieth not, and the fire is not quenched. (Mark 9:44)

And the angel of the Lord appeared unto him in a flame of fire out of the midst of a bush: and he looked, and, behold, the bush burned with fire, and the bush was not consumed. And Moses said, I will now turn aside, and see this great sight, why the bush is not burnt. (Exodus 3:2-3)

This eternal place is one of solitary confinement as well as complete darkness. It is a place of great never-ending pain and anguish in both the body, and the mind.

And cast ye the unprofitable servant into outer darkness: there shall be weeping and gnashing of teeth. (Matthew 25:30)

And shall cast them into the furnace of fire: there shall be wailing and gnashing of teeth.
(Matthew 13:50)

People who go to the Lake of Fire will be given bodies that will never die or burn up. They will feel the fire throughout their bodies, be in complete darkness they have never experienced, knowing in their minds there is no hope ever. Their mind will keep going over the events of their lives and everyone and everything that was around them. They are aware that they will never see them again, and the opportunities they had to receive Jesus as Savior and Lord but rejected Him. They will be tormented by the thought of the fact they gave up everything for a little bit of pleasure on earth, and how foolishly they acted.

This suffering will never cease; it is for eternity. The Lake of Fire is for those who have not received Jesus Christ as their Lord and Savior. Those who have received Jesus Christ as Lord and Savior will spend eternity in heaven.

To give you an idea of eternity, the following is an example. Take all the sand on the whole earth, including the USA and every country, and every year from all that sand take one grain and place it in the State of California. The next year take another grain, and place it with the first grain, until the very last grain is placed in one great pile.

Now consider, when you pick up a handful of sand, there are thousands of grains in just one handful which would be thousands of years just to place a handful in the State of California. The number of the grains of sand would be beyond our numbering system; this would be only the beginning of eternity and remember eternity has no ending. An eternity in the Lake of Fire is so horrible that it is beyond our comprehension. We cannot imagine it, and how terrible it will be for those who will go there.

Jesus said that He would go and prepare a place for us.

In my Father's house are many mansions: if it were not so, I would have told you. I go to prepare a place for you. And if I go and prepare a place for you, I will come again, and receive you unto myself; that where I am, there ye may be also. (John 14:2-3)

The other place where we can spend our eternity is Heaven. It is a place beyond our wildest dreams of beauty, peace, love, and fulfillment. The New Jerusalem, which God will descend to His Bride, the church, will be the place where we will dwell. The New Jerusalem is 1500 miles in every direction shaped like a cube.

AND I saw a new heaven and a new earth: for the first heaven and the first earth were passed away; and there was no more sea. And I John saw the holy city, new Jerusalem, coming down from God out of heaven, prepared as a bride adorned for her husband. And I heard a great voice out of heaven saying. Behold, the tabernacle of God is with men, and he will dwell with them, and they shall be his people, and God himself shall be with them, and be their God.

(Revelation 21:1-3)

This place will have the glory of God and cast a glorious light.

And he carried me away in the spirit to a great and high mountain, and shewed me that great city, the holy Jerusalem, descending out of heaven from God, (Revelation 21:10)

There will also be a pure river of the water of life.

AND he shewed me a pure river of water of life, clear as crystal, proceeding out of the throne of God and of the Lamb. In the midst of the street of it, and on either side of the river, was there the tree of life, which bare twelve manner of fruits, and yielded her fruit every month: and the leaves of the tree were for the healing of the nations. And there shall be no more curse: but the throne of God and of the Lamb shall be in it; and his servants shall serve him: And they shall see his face; and his name shall be in their foreheads. And there shall be no night there; and they need no candle, neither light of the sun; for the Lord God giveth them light: and they shall reign for ever and ever. (Revelation 22: 1-5)

On earth, we have gold, precious stones, and many beautiful, natural things like trees, flowers, and grass, but they are all just a dull image of what the real things are like in heaven. When we see the real things, they will be much more beautiful and colorful than the images that God gave us while we were here on earth. The colors will be more vivid, brighter and of a deeper hue than we have ever seen.

After Jesus returns for the church, we will be given a body like His.

After this I looked, and, behold, a door was opened in heaven: and the first voice which I heard was as it were of a trumpet talking with me; which said, Come up hither, and I will shew thee things which must be hereafter.

(Revelation 4:1)

Beloved, now are we the sons of God, and it doth not yet appear what we shall be: but we know that, when he shall appear, we shall be like him; for we shall see him as he is. (1 John 3:2)

In this new body we will not be limited, as Jesus walked through the closed door.

Then the same day at evening being the first day of the week, when the doors were shut where the disciples were assembled for fear of the Jews, came Jesus and stood in the midst, and saith unto them, Peace be unto you.... And after eight days again his disciples were within, and Thomas with them: then came Jesus, the doors being shut, and stood in the midst, and said, Peace be unto you. (John 20:19,26)

We will be able to eat, as Jesus did in His resurrected body.

Jesus then cometh, and taketh bread, and giveth them, and fish likewise. (John 21:13)

We also will be able to travel with no limitations. There will be no time in heaven similar to the timetable we follow here on earth. One thing that will make it heaven: The former things in our lives will be taken from us.

And God shall wipe away all tears from their eyes; and there shall be no more death, neither sorrow, nor crying, neither shall there be any more pain: for the former things are passed away. (Revelation 21:4)

There will be no night, no darkness and no need for the sunlight because God will give the light.

And there shall be no night there; and they need no candle, neither light of the sun; for the Lord God giveth them light: and they shall reign for ever and ever. (Revelation 22:5)

It is beyond our comprehension of what life will be like for the born-again child of God: No more getting old, because we will be ageless living in heavenly bliss for all eternity.

We will experience no more death, sickness, war, hate, lack of, or separation from the people and things we love that are there with us. Life will be perfection with everything beyond description forever present. We will suffer no bad times, no disturbing trials, and no difficult tests. The lamb will lay down with the lion, showing us that there will be nothing but love and peace in this place. God will be the source of everything. No longer will the devil be in our presence or be able to cause us problems.

And the devil that deceived them was cast into the lake of fire and brimstone, where the beast and the false prophet are, and shall be tormented day and night for ever and ever.

(Revelation 20:10)

My wife and I have parents, family, and friends who are in Heaven, whom we really miss and always long to see them. To my wife and I, the greatest thing about going to Heaven is seeing Jesus face-to-face, which will be a greater experience than everything else put together. It is all about Jesus and living with Him forever. What a glorious thought.

I have given you a short description of Heaven and the Lake of Fire, two places where all mankind has a choice of where they will spend their eternity. If you knew that you only had one day to live what would be most important to you? I do not think it would be your job, money, retirement, vacation, or anything else in this world. I would want to honestly know where I was going, when I die. Jesus made it possible for us to know about our final destination.

These things have I written unto you that believe on the name of the Son of God; that ye may know that ye have eternal life, and that ye may believe on the name of the Son of God.

(1 John 5:13)

God gave His Son Jesus as a gift to all mankind that we may believe in Him and have eternal life.

For God so loved the world, that he gave his only begotten Son that whosoever believeth in him should not perish, but have everlasting life.

(John 3:16)

We first must believe that we are sinners.

As it is written, There is none righteous, no, not one: (Romans 3:10)

For all have sinned, and come short of the glory of God; (Romans 3:23)

We also must realize that God sent Jesus to die for us.

But God commendeth his love toward us, in that, while we were yet sinners, Christ died for us. (Romans 5:8)

We then repent (turn away from our sin) and ask Jesus to forgive us, to come into our hearts and be Savior and Lord of our lives.

That if thou shalt confess with thy mouth the Lord Jesus, and shalt believe in thine heart that God hath raised him from the dead, thou shalt be saved. For with the heart man believeth unto righteousness; and with the mouth confession is made unto salvation... For whosoever shall call upon the name of the Lord shall be saved.

(Romans 10:9,10,13)

If we accept the above-noted facts and their meaning in our hearts, and not treat them as just words out of our mouth, we are saved. Our names will be written in the Lamb's Book of Life and our destination will be changed from hell to heaven.

Verily, verily, I say unto you. He that heareth my word, and believeth on him that sent me, hath everlasting life, and shall not come into condemnation; but is passed from death unto life.

(John 5:24)

A Prayer for Salvation

Heavenly Father God, I come to You in the name of Jesus Christ. I am a sinner and believe that Jesus died for my sins, was buried, and arose from the dead. Father God, I repent and turn away from my sins and ask You to forgive me and cleanse away all my sins with the Blood of the Lamb Jesus Christ. I receive Jesus Christ as my Savior and Lord of my life from this time forth. Jesus, You are Lord of my life and I thank You, Lord, for saving me in Jesus' Name. Amen.

If you meant this prayer in your heart, you are saved, because whoever calls upon the name of the Lord shall be saved.

For whosoever shall call upon the name of the Lord, shall be saved. (Romans 10:13)

Just believe it by faith and confess your salvation to those around you. As you tell others, pray, and read your Bible starting with the Gospel of John, and apply God's Word to your life. As time passes, He will become more and more real to you.

A Prayer for Rededication to God

Heavenly Father God, I give my life to You, and ask that You forgive me of my sins, selfish ways, and disobedience to You. I ask You to cleanse away all my sins with the Blood of the Lamb Jesus Christ. I return back to You and ask You to fill me with Your Holy Spirit, and empower me to serve You and to be obedient to You in all things. I know that You have a plan for my life, and I want You to fulfill that plan. I give You my life now to use as a vessel for Your Glory. I ask You to help me live a godly life for You, and for me to be an example to others and bring many into the Kingdom for You, Lord. Thank You, Lord for hearing my prayer and anointing me for Your service in Jesus' Name. Amen.

Conclusion

Before writing this last part of my book, the Conclusion, God gave me the title that He wanted me to use for this book. I would like to share with you the title name and the revelation that He gave me about the title of my book, "OVERPOWERING INFLUENCE OF THE TRUTH".

The word OVERPOWERING in the dictionary means to furnish with more power than is needed, overwhelm, to overcome or master by superior force: to overpower an enemy, furnish too much power, unbearable, and irresistible. INFLUENCE means power that produces effects, a compelling force, the ability to produce effects indirectly by means of power based on high position. TRUTH means reality, correctness, actual existence, that which is true, an established or verified fact.

Putting it together is this: first of all there is OVERPOWERING so strong that it causes effects in everyone with whom it comes in contact, without forcing or being forceful, when it is God's Word which is God's truth. The INFLUENCE will be unbearable to those that reject it and irresistible to those that will receive it. Our Free Will to accept or reject. TRUTH is God and His Word to us, The Bible. God's Word is alive and will bring results wherever it goes to those that will receive it by faith.

So shall my word be that goeth forth out of my mouth: it shall not return unto me void, but it shall accomplish that which I please, and it shall prosper in the thing whereto I sent it.

(Isaiah 55:11)

I have tried to show the readers that whenever you apply the Bible to your life in any area that is backed up by the scripture and do what it says, you will get the results that it promises.

The most powerful Overpowering Influence on the earth is the Love of God. God's Love is the motivation by which all things were created and the reality that of all things are possible for God to do and accomplish in our lives. The Overpowering Influence of God negates all the works of Satan and evil influence, when we apply God's Word to any situation in our lives that needs to be corrected.

There is a pathway on which God's love leads us, one that was provided for us when Jesus shed His blood for us at Calvary, died, was buried, and resurrected, giving us God's plan of salvation

For the grace of God that bringeth salvation hath appeared to all men, (Titus 2:11)

When we ask forgiveness for our sins and make Jesus Christ our Lord and Savior, we are born again and are given all things that pertain to life and godliness that we need in this life and life eternal in heaven.

According as his divine power hath given unto us all things that pertain unto life and godliness, through the knowledge of him that hath called us to glory and virtue: Whereby are given unto us exceeding great and precious promises: that by these ye might be partakers of the divine nature, having escaped the corruption that is in the world through lust. (2 Peter 1:3-4)

Our journey and pathway begin at this point, and Jesus will continue this good work in us until we leave this earth.

Being confident of this very thing, that he which hath begun a good work in you will perform it until the day of Jesus Christ.

(Philippians 1:6)

We are to be faithful to the Lord in our walk with Him, as long as we live on this earth.

Moreover it is required in stewards, that a man be found faithful. (1 Corinthians 4:2)

God intends for us to reflect His Son Jesus Christ to a lost and dying world by our lifestyle, actions, words, and deeds, and to be overcomers of life's obstacles that challenge us. I have seen so many Christians living defeated lives and having little affect on those around them; this was a deep motivation to me in writing this book.

The Holy Spirit led me to write about different subjects, many of my personal experiences with God's Word, how He gave me the victory in my life and caused me to be effective to others in the ministry to which God called me. Healing, miracles and getting people set free have been major parts of my ministry. I have a strong passion for seeing people set free by the power of God. If we know the truth, it will make us free.

And ye shall know the truth, and the truth shall make you free. (John 8:32)

Through this book I have given the ingredients that will lead us to an abundant, overcoming, and fruitful life for the Lord.

My prayer is that all the readers will let the Holy Spirit direct them on how and when they apply the many truths of God's Word in this book into their lives, and thus, will live abundant, overcoming, and fruitful lives in Jesus Christ.

About the Author

I was born and raised in Chambersburg, a historical town in Pennsylvania. Chambersburg is located twenty-six miles from Gettysburg, a major Civil War site. I was an only child of a loving family who had only a meager income. They attended church but were not devoted Christians. At that time, they had not accepted Jesus Christ as their personal Savior.

The pastor of the church where we attended taught us about Jesus Christ, but I did not know Him as my personal Savior. My grandparents were Christians and taught me a little about Christianity during my childhood. So, basically, I was in the dark spiritually until adulthood.

I graduated from Chambersburg Area Senior High School in 1962, joined the US Army in October 1962 and served in the military for three years. In 1966 I met a beautiful young lady, who later became my wife.

Sabina and I were married July 8, 1967 and lived together for three years as husband and wife before committing our lives to Jesus Christ. In the living room of our own home, we repented of our sins and were saved. The pastor and his wife, who were visiting in our home, led us to the Lord Jesus Christ. Our lives changed dramatically through the Holy Spirit and shortly thereafter, we were able to lead our parents to the Lord.

I totally committed to serving the Lord Jesus Christ; I began searching the Scriptures of the Holy Bible for truth and guidance. My desire was to minister and win lost souls into the Kingdom of God. I was ordained into the ministry in September 1975 by the State Superintendent and several other ministers in the Association of Fundamental Ministers and Churches. It was a very unique evening with the leaders of the AFMC members and friends present for my Ordination. They told me that I was scheduled to preach that evening just forty-five minutes away from the time they told me. It would have been a great challenge for me if I had not been prepared ahead of time. But the Lord came to me the night before and told me to prepare my message for the Service. So, I was prepared and ready to speak for the Lord. God is faithful in my life by ordering my steps so I will not stumble and fall!

The training for my ministry has been through Church Seminars, Bible courses, and working with many pastors. But the greatest teacher has been the Holy Spirit, speaking to me and guiding me in the ways of all truth. After receiving Christ as my Lord and Savior, I was overwhelmed by the size of the Bible; it frightened me. I said, "Lord, please help me learn your Word." And He did.

I spent approximately ten hours a day reading the Word of God and praying to the Holy Spirit for comprehension to understand its meaning. God gave me Scriptures to memorize and to learn where they were located in the Bible. He was fulfilling my request to learn His

Word, but I had to do my part and co-operate with Him. God has given me the ability to quote Scriptures and know where they are located, knowledge which helps me in preaching, teaching and counseling. I have gotten much revelation from God. He has done some very unique things in and through my ministry and for my family which I have shared in this book.

In the service to my Lord I have held different positions in the ministry. Each one of these positions has given me great rewards in the Kingdom of God. I have been an Adult Sunday School Teacher, Deacon, Prayer Leader, and Usher for the Church. I was also involved with the Bus Ministry and Children's Ministry. It was a very rewarding experience for me to be active in Child Evangelism through Children's Bible School and Youth Camp with a local church.

I was the pastor for a pioneer church for the "Church of God" in Maryland and also started several churches. I was part of a street ministry in Charlotte, North Carolina, where I preached, taught, counseled and fed the people.

I was involved with the Morris Cerullo Ministries as Telephone Supervisor plus teaching and serving weekly communion. I also served in the capacity as counselor, evangelist, and trained men and women for the service of the Lord.

I love God and people with all my heart, and my passion is to show them who Jesus Christ really is and not how He is portrayed by so many others. I want people to have the understanding that they can receive God's Promises and serve Him in the calling He has for their lives.

If I can encourage and teach others the truth through the Scriptures in the Holy Bible, then I can connect them to the True Vine who is Christ Jesus; that is my purpose for writing this book.

My wife and I work together in a healing and miracle ministry. Our ministry is the Gospel of Jesus Christ in salvation, healing and deliverance. The greatest miracle is Salvation which is the purpose of our ministry—to bring lost souls into the Kingdom of God. We have seen and experienced many miracles of God through the years in our lives and ministry and want to share these wonderful experiences with you. Every experience is backed up with the Word of God. God has given me and my family His Mercy and Grace and has blessed us with great favor.

When in school I hated public speaking class, reading and writing. I soon learned these three things are "a must" in order for a minister to succeed. God completely turned me around and gave me the ability to do all three. I am amazed at what He has done in my life.

My writing started on the Internet through the social networking of Facebook. I posted teachings and Scriptures from the Holy Bible to help others. God used a godly lady to encourage me to continue to post words of encouragement, because the Lord was touching many people through the posts. Another godly lady, a successful writer with several Christian books on the market, saw my posts and was impressed at my writing ability. She suggested that I should write a book to help others in their walk of faith in the Lord Jesus Christ. Through her encouragement of my ability, I started writing this book. She assured me that she would guide me through the procedures of writing the manuscript until it is in book form and published. I can see how God is using me to write and say things that I know are from Him. It amazes me how God has enabled me to write words that can change people's lives through the Holy Spirit.

I give great love and true respect to my devoted and lovely wife who has always been my best friend and eager encourager. I love you, Sabina. With the support and help from the Most High God, my lovely wife and my 'Sister in Christ' my writing mentor – I believe this wonderful book will touch the hearts of many people in this world for Jesus Christ. This belief is my goal and passion.

Edward Franklin Eberly

Minister – Evangelist – Pastor
Motivational Speaker
Writer – Author

Edward Eberly is available for revivals, speaking engagements, and miracle services operating in the Gifts of the Holy Spirit. In his services, he has witnessed many miracle healings and deliverances by the Power of the Holy Spirit. His greatest passion is for lost souls to be saved by our Lord and Savior Jesus Christ and teaching them how to live a successful life by growing spiritually in the Kingdom of God.

Edward is a great motivational speaker and welcomes the opportunity to speak at Men's Business Meetings and Men's Conferences. He is well qualified to teach young Ministers, Evangelists, and Pastors the interpretation of the overpowering influence of the truth in God's Word and how to be the best in their calling for the Gospel of Jesus Christ.

Edward's goal is to reach the world with the Gospel of Jesus Christ through the Radio, the Media (Internet and Television), Books, Churches, Men's Business Meetings, and Conferences.

Contact Edward Franklin Eberly at:
Email: extendedhandsofjesus@yahoo.com
Website: www.extendedhandsofjesus.org

www.ingramcontent.com/pod-product-compliance
Lightning Source LLC
Chambersburg PA
CBHW030923090426
42737CB00007B/300